FINANCIAL

PEACE

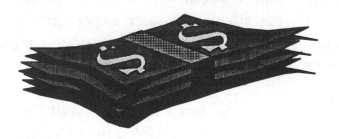

BY DAVID L. RAMSEY III

Published by *LAMPO Press*

Cover Design By Julie Kobielush

TABLE OF CONTENTS

DEDICATION

I am dedicating this book to my wonderful wife Sharon, who stuck it out while I learned all these lessons the hard way. She has embodied the truth that real love is commitment, even when it is not fun. Thank-you honey, I love you.

ACKNOWLEDGMENTS

I wish to thank all those people who have inspired me through the task of a first book. When you have lived as much of this material as we have, writing this was somewhat like birthing a child.

My friends and pastors at Christ Church Nashville, thank-you for being my editors, readers, and examples of how we are all supposed to walk before the Lord.

My parents, whose entrepreneurial spirit, when given to me has always told me to get up and go on.

My Lord Jesus, for the power and mercy that you have shown in my life and most of all for your grace without which I would be lost.

ABOUT THE AUTHOR:

Dave Ramsey was born in East Tennessee, and raised in Nashville. After receiving a B.S. in Finance and Real Estate at the University of Tennessee, he went on to found Ramsey Investments, Inc. a real estate brokerage firm specializing in foreclosure and bankruptcy real estate. He is also the founder of Lampo Consulting, a consulting firm founded to do bankruptcy avoidance counseling. During the eight years of counseling and foreclosure brokerage he has reviewed over ten thousand foreclosure situations and done in depth counseling for several hundred families.

Dave has been married for over ten years to his wonderful wife Sharon, and is the proud father of two girls, Denise and Rachel, and one boy, Daniel.

He has over 14 years experience as a real estate broker during which time he has accumulated several titles, including being one of Tennessee's youngest brokers to be admitted to the Graduate Realtors Institute. He is Vice-President of the Nashville Real Estate Investors. He is licensed to sell life, health, and disability insurance and has held mortgage brokers and securities licenses. Dave is currently also the host of a popular talk radio show in Nashville dealing with financial matters.

By the age of 26 Dave had accumulated over four million dollars in real estate. He then lost his entire portfolio and virtually everything he owned. He has now rebuilt his financial life, but that experience combined with years of counseling gives him an unusually deep perspective and insight into money matters as well as a comprehensive look into the foreclosure and bankruptcy scene.

PREFACE

The speaker asked the people to raise the envelope containing their bills over their heads to pray for their financial predicaments. With a twinkle in his eye he said for those with boxes to be careful not to strain their backs. He then prayed over their bills asking God to remove the bondage that these financial predicaments had brought to their lives. Then came the most significant part.

After the prayer he asked everyone, even the distinguished businessman, even the society lady, everyone, to make the noise that they will make the day that they are no longer in debt or are completely cleared of their financial predicament. I heard a roar and a celebration come from those one thousand people that would rival the Super Bowl. People of *every* area of life were celebrating the mere thought of being financially free. It was like few expressions of joy I have ever witnessed. Just when I thought they were slowing and going to quiet down another wave of celebration crossed the hall.

I had been sitting in a meeting on personal finance held in a local church. This experience helped reiterate to me the amount of pain we, the American people, are in regarding our personal finances. I had been researching and living this book for four years at that point. What I witnessed put an emotional reminder in me that we as a people have got to get a handle on our finances. *It is time.* It is time we started controlling our money, instead of money, or the lack of money, controlling us! The celebration I witnessed that night was merely a reflection of what I have seen as a paralyzing cancer that is rampant in our country.

You may think that this was merely some religious emotionalism. However, let me assure you that after having counseled hundreds of people through financial crises that a huge percentage, even a scary percentage, of the American public at large would throw an unprecedented nationwide celebration if they could simply get control of their finances. And there is a way . . .

CHAPTER ONE

THE BEGINNING,
A VERY GOOD PLACE TO START

As I stood putting gas in my Jaguar, the cold damp January wind chilled me, and seemed to dampen my spirits even more. I hoped the attendant inside would not run a telephone check on my Gold Card. If he did they probably would turn me down. Then where would I be? "This is ridiculous" I thought, "Only in America could you drive a Jaguar and not have the money to put gas in it." I wondered where the arrogant young man was from a few years earlier. There I stood in the cold, a young man in my twenties, knowing I was in the process of losing virtually everything I owned. Yet, it had not always been that way.

After college I hit a couple of minor bumps in my career, but found a niche in foreclosure bargain real estate. With a formal education in finance, a family background in real estate, and a burning desire to succeed I had a head start on life. As my real estate business grew everything I touched seemed to turn to gold. I began to collect rental properties, as well as buy and sell bargain properties. I was very good at it and made money quickly. By age 26 my rental real estate portfolio was worth in excess of four million dollars. I had built a team of people to manage this growing company and everything was moving perfectly. Or so I thought. My wife and I did all the exotic vacations, drove the top name autos, and wore only expensive custom tailored suits. You may be able to imagine that for a young man of 26, I thought I had it made.

FINANCIAL INDEPENDENCE ?

I had arrived at "financial independence"; that mystical place every young entrepreneur wants get to. If I wanted something. I bought it. No thought required. I had done it honestly, with hard work and intelligence. So what could possibly happen in paradise?

Along with my knack for obtaining bargains, I had another talent. I had an unusual ability to finance everything. If one of my business lines of credit ran low, I would put on my custom suit, get in my Jaguar and head for the bank. I would make sure to park in front of the managers window for a big impression. I had my financial statements, corporate strategy, and tax returns all bound for presentation. All this pomp and circumstance, combined with the fact that my "deals" always worked, enamored the bankers, and they loved to lend me money. We had every type of personal line of credit, business lines of credit, equity lines of credit, and don't forget those wonderful Gold and Platinum Cards.

If a banker would dare to indicate I might have too much debt, I would hunt another source. I have taken a $20,000 draw on a line of credit in a cashier's check, walked out of that bank and into another. With all the "presentation" explained above and a $20,000 cashiers check I would "establish a new relationship." Which meant I would deposit my borrowed cash into their bank, promise to be a customer, and in return they would give me a new $100,000 line of credit plus every Platinum Card and personal line of credit they had.

The sarcastic way that I am explaining this to you almost makes the process seem immoral. However, we were making money, and had a bright future, so the banks wanted customers like us.

ALL GOOD THINGS COME TO AN END

Then it happened. Our largest lender was sold to a larger bank. Neither pomp and circumstance, nor my name, meant anything to the new upper management. Also, the 1986 tax act began to have its negative impact on real estate so all the banks began to get worried. Upper management decided to "trim back" on real estate lending. Most of our borrowing was in short term notes because we resold most of our property for profit. Because they were "open lines of credit" and short term notes they had the right to call most our debt within 90 days. And THAT is just what they did. The new management called all my notes.

I had 90-days to find 1.2 million dollars. I paid virtually all of it, but doing so destroyed my business. That action started a chain reaction that ended in my losing everything, but my home and the clothes on my back.

I remember the strain on my marriage, I remember the mornings standing in the shower with the water scalding my face and crying like a baby. I remember the Sheriff serving the lawsuit papers for default on notes. I remember thinking of suicide, knowing I had a one million dollar life insurance policy that would provide for my family better than I was.

It took three and one half years for paradise to completely unravel and for me to end up broke. From the nightmare and emotional pain was born an idea. The idea of counseling the average consumer through debt problems. I found that the foreclosure experience I had, combined with my personal experience with financial pain, was a foundation for opening a consulting company to counsel consumers. I attended any and every workshop or seminar available and devoured every book I could find on consumer financial problems.

The Beginning . . .

I opened that company and ran it for some time dealing with several hundred cases of consumer counseling on financial crisis. The base of knowledge from that experience is partially what I draw this material from.

ENOUGH PAIN ALREADY !

Having lived through that trepidation, sat with countless others while they lived through the same horrors of financial stress, and after watching over 10,000 foreclosures come across my desk in ten years, I have had enough! It is time we Americans get a handle on our finances. We have been Gomer Pyleing it through our lives long enough. Down South we call this ridiculous walk down apathy lane in a Valium state of mind "ditty bopping along."

I believe it is time for the typical American family to get out of financial bondage. I also believe that they are ready. Furthermore, I believe through knowledge and discipline *financial peace* is possible for us, all of us.

CHAPTER TWO

ENOUGH OF ANYTHING IS
TOO MUCH

The American consumer is facing dire financial straits. The story outlined for you in the last chapter and the hundreds of families I have counseled leads me to that conclusion. In observing national trends and the information gathered by hands-on observation over the past ten years I am disturbed by the direction our personal management of money has taken.

Our nation's financial situation with record budget deficits and bank failures is deplorable. However, the nation's situation is only a reflection of our personal failures in our inability to "Just Say No" to ourselves. Our inability to get control of financial matters in our personal lives will have to be solved before we can demand accountability from elected officials. Our spoiled Congress is only a reflection of our spoiled selves. The good of our country is overlooked so our pet special interest groups can be served just like the good of the family is often

We must have one that tells the time in Japan while simultaneously taping soap operas in Afghanistan three weeks from now! We cannot be content to own a refrigerator to keep food from rotting, we must have one that talks and makes sandwiches at half-time. I am not criticizing owning nice things because I own *"stuff."* But, I am saying we have stressed our family budgets and are crashing ourselves by buying all this *"stuff"* before we can really afford it.

Our businesses have followed the same general change in philosophy. Businesses used to believe in having high cash reserves, but now most are run on a shoe string, with no provision for the cycles that *do* come. They now believe in joint ventures, leveraged buyouts (which simply means the entire purchase is on borrowed funds, which usually strains the company to an unhealthy position), and the heavy use of capital markets of all kinds. Consequently, in the last few years we have seen the highest rate of business failure ever. The volatility brought on by business failures has rippled through every part of our lives, spreading insecurity, fear, and actual financial, spiritual, and emotional damage.

The American family has especially felt the effects of these changes in our financial philosophy. The very core of the family is dramatically affected by this over-buying which creates over-borrowing. Most marriages that fail list financial problems as a contributing factor, if not the main reason for the failure. Marriages of 25 years or more are many times destroyed by foreclosure or bankruptcy. Their *"stuff"* must have owned them instead of them owning their *"stuff."*

Our entire nation is in financial stress at the individual level, at the city and state level and at the national level. We have been having "Fun Fun Fun til daddy takes the T-bird away." Are you depressed yet? I hope so. I intend in this chapter not to give you a guilt trip nor simply to leave you hopeless, but instead to get you mad. Get you mad enough to change your life, and mad enough to change your children's lives. Maybe even mad enough to change your city or your country.

MAD IS NOT THE WORD FOR IT

I have had enough! Enough living in bondage to *"stuff."* Enough of having a bank collector, credit card collector, or mortgage company call and ruin my evening with those collection calls. I finally got sick and tired of it! And when I got sick and tired of being sick and tired, I decided to learn something about money, how it works, how it *really* works, and how to work it. I decided to learn the things not taught in college finance class. I decided because of losing virtually everything I owned that I was tired of living in stress due to money or the lack of money.

After counseling for several years, I am still mad. I am tired of seeing my friends divorce over money problems. I am tired of having grown men and women in my office with thoughts of suicide as they lose everything they own. I am tired of seeing single moms work 70 hour weeks just to try to make a living and simply put food on the table. I am tired of watching our Congress and President pass more trillion dollar deficits.

Is there hope? Absolutely, but we must shift our view of *"stuff,"* money, and how to handle it. I see dramatic things happen to people who apply simple and forgotten principles to all areas of their life. You can turn your personal financial problems and challenges into opportunities in just a few weeks. You can redirect your entire life within just a short period of time. I am even optimistic that our nation can and will be saved by a return to simple basic principles that have been taught and lived since Old Testament times. If you need more peace in your financial life finish this book. As I said in the Preface, there is a way . . .

CHAPTER THREE

THE BASICS (A FOUNDATION)

We Americans, with all our bad habits, are not necessarily bad people. The people who have come to me for crisis financial counseling and those who come to me that are being foreclosed on are not evil people. They are not scammers or schemers that got caught and are going to jail as soon as they lose their home. These people in trouble are in your family. They work with you, they live on your street, and sometimes they are you. I have seldom met anyone who set out with a plan to defraud creditors or steal money by borrowing and not paying it back. Then what gets people in trouble if not their lack of morals?

We as a culture are ignorant of what money is and how to handle it. Ignorance is not lack of intelligence, it is lack of knowledge on a particular subject. If I were put in a chemistry lab I would probably blow something up, but I am not unintelligent. I am ignorant of chemistry. If you needed brain surgery I doubt you would use me, not because I am unintelligent, but because I am ignorant of brain surgery and its processes.

HOW CAN THIS BE?

It is almost impossible to get out of high school today without knowing what an amoeba is or without having read some of the great literary works, but few high school seniors can keep a checkbook balanced. They are taught virtually nothing about the real world of money. I am not talking about money on Wall Street. I am talking about money on your street. We are not taught basic principles of managing and making financial decisions for our own family.

Consequently we come out of high school or even College and set up housekeeping. We don't have knowledge of leases, but we sign one. We don't have knowledge of cars and car financing, but we buy one and sign the loan papers. We don't have knowledge of the implications of credit cards and high interest rates, but we get five pre-approved cards in the first two years out of school and so we use them. We don't know about Rule of 78's or prepayment penalties so we finance our waterbeds, stereos, TVs, and washer and dryers. It was all so innocent and happened so slowly that the monster in the closet was not noticeable.

THE FAMOUS FIVE YEAR MARK

After about five years of marriage the average couple begins to feel pinched in the pocketbook. They have little or no savings and start to get scared. They may get scared enough to curb spending for about six months, but then go back to their old ways and still end up in trouble very quickly. All of this could have been prevented by some basic knowledge.

In my counseling of the "average" couple, I found their problem to simply be a lack of knowledge and discipline. I have found that money has two properties that most people don't acknowledge or understand.

VERY ACTIVE

First, MONEY IS ACTIVE. Finance and money are always moving. Time, interest rates, amounts, cash flows, inflation, and risk all intermingle to create a current that is ever flowing. Whether you choose to impact these currents is irrelevant, they still go on. If you took $10,000 and buried it in the back yard for ten years will it buy as much when you dig it up as it will now? Obviously not. We must learn that the current or flow of the mathematical process is always affecting our money. It NEVER stops. Money in this sense is like a beautiful thoroughbred horse, very powerful and always moving in action, but if you don't train this horse when it is very young, you will have an out-of-control and dangerous animal on your hands when he grows to maturity.

The point is: *"You must gain control over your finances or they will gain control over you."*

If you don't take action continually on your money, it or the lack of it will take action on you. Finance is not passive. It REQUIRES you to take the initiative to control it.

AMORAL- NO MORALS

Second, MONEY IS AMORAL. Money has no morals. That is, it is neither good nor bad. The Bible in I Timothy 6:10 does not say "Money is the root of all evil." What it does say is " The *love* of money is the root of all evil." Money in and of itself has no more moral quality than a brick. So just because you are poor does not mean that you are good or spiritually superior; neither does it mean that you are bad or spiritually inferior. On the other hand if you are wealthy it does not mean that you are inherently good or spiritually superior, nor does it mean that you are a crook, or a bad person, or spiritually inferior. You decide what you are. The way you act through your money or your lack of it will show us whether YOU are good or evil, but the money itself is neither.

WHERE IS YOUR VALUE?

Be careful of a society that will give you your value as a person based upon it's wrong view of collecting *"stuff"*. Your value as a human being, as a person, is not based on your ability to collect *"stuff"*. If you have jumped on this train of thought, you will be derailed because the first principle mentioned will get you. Money is "Active" in the philosophical realm as well. When your priorities get off track money will take command instantly because of it's active principle.

Money is simply a non-entity that must be manipulated. The better we are at manipulating it the more of it we will control. Until we take this "Active" and "Amoral" view of money it will continue to have the upper hand in every part of our lives.

I have developed and absorbed ideas of personal financial control from much experience and study of experts on this subject. I claim little originality in any of these philosophies, but simply offer a new presentation of these ideas in a different format. Pain is a very permanent teacher and I have lived through financial disaster and viewed much pain in others. I have drawn from this background to develop for you a track that you can run your finances on. *Financial Peace* and *"the peace puppies"* introduced in the next chapter were developed to help you look at where you are and where you want to be. None of these principles will work in the least if you don't work them, but if you do work them these principles will lead you directly to financial peace. *Do* pass go, *do* collect your $200.

Good Luck!

CHAPTER FOUR

UNDERSTAND THE SPIRITUAL ASPECTS OF MONEY

There are those who believe that finance is merely an exact mathematical science. That is the way it is taught in the universities. Finance is, in fact, an exact mathematical science until a human touches it. Personal finance is who you are. The personal, philosophical, and emotional problems and strengths that you have will be reflected in your use of money. If you are very disciplined you can be a good saver of money. If you are very selfish or self-centered you will surround yourself with expensive toys that you cannot afford.

THE CHARACTER OF MONEY

Larry Burkett, a noted author on this subject of money, says money problems are normally not the problem, but instead the symptom of a personal short fall. My experience in counseling with people confirms Burkett's statement. *Extreme amounts of money or extreme lack of it magnifies character.* A person not committed totally to honesty will tell white lies and sometimes even commit fraud by lying on a loan application when money is tight.

Doug Parsons, in his sermon entitled "A Life Above The Ordinary", tells an interesting story about character. One of the richest and most powerful men in America owns a huge company which consists of thousands of employees. This gentleman pointed out an up and coming low level manager to his upper level staff. The young man pointed out worked very hard and was very good at his management position. The owner noticed the young man because of his work ethic and talent and commented that someday this young man would be a regional manager long before his time. Sure enough, the young man continued to work hard and be promoted up through the ranks to the point that the next promotion was to be the regional manager promotion. When the owner became aware that this promotion was to be made he decided to fly down and give the promotion personally over lunch.

So the big day arrived and the owner flew in to take the young man to lunch. But as the young man and the owner were going through the cafeteria style line for lunch the owner noticed the young man very deliberately hide a one cent pat of butter under his roll so as not to be charged for it. The lunch went fine except no promotion was given and when the owner returned to his offices he had the young man fired. Not only did the young man miss a several hundred thousand dollar per year position, but even lost his job.

A close friend of mine suggested that such an extreme action was a bit severe. Maybe the warmth of the roll was to warm the butter making it easy to spread? Whatever the other circumstances surrounding the story were, the story still makes the point that the owner understood that the character flaw of dishonesty would be magnified under pressure and like a weak spot in an inner tube would eventually blow out.

WHAT WE DO SHOWS WHO WE ARE

We have all seen someone get rich overnight through a lottery or inheritance, and because of their immaturity, blow the entire fortune in the twinkle of an eye. On the other hand, I have seen people who grew as an individual more during a financial crisis than at anytime in their lives. Sometimes we see people get wealthy and it magnifies the good character they had within. Steel magnate Andrew Carnegie, a very well known philanthropist and humanitarian, spent the first half of his life attaining wealth and the last half of his life giving it away. Many of the libraries across our nation were established by his donated funds. Many other famous philanthropists have shown us that their good character was merely magnified by their attainment of wealth. Perhaps St. Ambrose said it best when he said "Just as riches are an impediment to virtue in the wicked, so in the good they are an aid of virtue."

STUFFITIS - A DEADLY DISEASE

We Americans like *"stuff"*. We have been called materialistic, self centered, the "me" generation. I have never liked being accused of being materialistic, but admittedly I do like good *"stuff"*. I like good cars, expensive food, nice clothes, and very large houses, but I am not materialistic. I am guilty of having contracted a disease known as *"Stuffitis"* where the bearer has an insatiable desire for only *"GOOD STUFF"*. If you have *"stuffitis"* you might look like you are materialistic, but the difference is you will not collect just anything, only the good *"stuff."* Please do not confuse "the good *"stuff""* with "the right stuff" which stands for internal courage and quick reactions that a great fighter pilot must have. I am not the only one that has *"stuffitis"*, I see people all the time who have it. There is no cure for this disease called *"stuffitis,"* but we will discuss more ways to control it in later chapters.

One of the ways you can spot *"stuffitis"* in its later stages is to see people who have gotten confused and have not put money in its proper priority. The Bible story in Exodus 32 of Moses coming down off of Mount Sinai after receiving the Ten Commandments gives us insight. What were the people doing that angered him so? Worshiping a golden calf - *"stuffitis"*. When we forget that our money is not to be our Creator, that instead we are supposed to create with it, we wreak havoc in our lives. Our forefathers may not have meant to, but they put a reminder on our currency to avoid *"stuffitis"*, "In God We Trust." Please notice it did not say "In *"Stuff"* We Trust." We must keep money and the handling of it in proper perspective. Do not treat it carelessly, for this collecting of *"stuff"* is only a game of Monopoly.

INDEPENDENT OF WHAT ?

We Americans have developed the concept in the last 30 years that we all want to be "Financially Independent." Independent of what!? Can you gain enough money that you never have to worry or be cautious again? Can you gain enough money that you can protect your family from injury or sickness? Can you accumulate enough money to be guaranteed you won't lose everything due to war, famine, or financial markets collapsing? I have never read about or met anyone who could horde this much money. You can be a better manager and gain more control and peace in the handling of finance, but you can never be totally independent as long as you are alive. Money is ACTIVE and you must keep managing it and moving it no matter how much you attain. You can (and I expect you to) do well in handling your money and you should try to gain as much as is in your ability, but do not let this pursuit become all consuming. Be careful of spending all your energy and time trying to reach "Financial Independence" because this nonexistent place is as nonexistent as the god of that golden calf.

THE DIRTY WORD

We have discussed how the strengths and weaknesses in your life will affect your personal finances and we cannot leave that subject without dealing with one of life's dirtiest words. *Discipline.* You will have conflict, worry, shortages, and general lack of fun until you achieve some discipline in the handling of your funds. I am not saying you have to run, or live in, a financial boot camp, but you must start to plug in your brain before you sign that check. You must begin today to look at your finances differently than you ever have before. Recognize they will be totally under your control, if you will merely take the reigns.

TO GIVE OR NOT TO GIVE?

The last spiritual aspect you must understand is "farming." No farmer has ever grown a crop unless he planted some seed. Personal growth requires that you give money away. The institutions you give to will survive if you don't, but you will have missed an opportunity to benefit. If you feel like you don't have enough to give start by giving small amounts and by giving of your time, but give something. You must decide that while you are important, the universe does not hinge on your particular challenges or on you. Somehow giving reminds us of that and that no matter what your financial status is there is always someone much worse off. There are things set in motion in your life and your finances when you give that cannot be calculated or quantified. I have seen many couples make the turn towards financial peace simply by adhering to this principle.

You need to plant some seed in self growth and you can do this only by giving. I do not totally understand what giving does to the human spirit, but I do know that I meet very few well-balanced, happy, healthy, wealthy people who don't give money away.

Beware of who you give to and what they do with the money. Beware does not mean being cynical because there are no perfect institutions, but be responsible with your giving. John Wesley said "Make all you can, save all you can, give all you can." Giving helps us keep proper priorities in our lives and it is essential to good money management.

Christians should give tithes to their local church. I will not expand in depth as that detail is not my purpose here, but instead list these scripture references for those interested:

I Chronicles 26:20   Genesis 14:18-20
Malachi 3:7-12   I Corinthians 9:7
Matthew 23:23 & Luke 11:42
"These things you should do...

JUST A MATTER OF MATH?

In conclusion, to think that the handling of your personal finances is merely a matter of math control is naive. You must get better control of all aspects of your life. Until you do, the next chapters while having some effect, will be neutralized by the other habits in your life. If you drink until it affects your finances, get help. If you do drugs or compulsively do ANYTHING that affects your finances this is a sure sign you are an addict. Please seek counseling. I am not able through any amount of knowledge presented in the following chapters to help you overcome problems at that level.

Please spend five minutes at the close of this chapter quietly looking into yourself. Then write down the resolutions of change, minor or major, that you see you must make. We are going to have some fun and learn a lot about finally getting control.

I am your constant companion,
I am your greatest helper or your heaviest burden.
I will push you onward or drag you down to failure.
I am at your command.
Half of the tasks that you do you might just as well
turn over to me and I will do them quickly and
correctly.

I am easily managed, you must merely be firm with
me, Show me exactly how you want something
done;
After a few lessons I will do it automatically.
I am the servant of all great people and alas of all
failures as well.
Those who are great I have made great,
Those who are failures I have made failures.

I am not a machine, but I work with all the precision
of a machine, plus the intelligence of a person.
Now you may run me for profit or you may run me
for ruin. It makes no difference to me.
Take me, Train me, be firm with me, and I will lay
the world at your feet.
Be easy with me and I will destroy you.

WHO AM I ? .... I AM CALLED HABIT.

*I discovered this little gem at a seminar a few years
ago and it applies here.   Author unknown.*

I would like to introduce you to "Peace Puppies." Peace Puppies meet Reader, Reader meet Peace Puppies. These are principles which must be applied to your life with discipline. I will develop these principled puppies throughout the balance of the book.

These are great creatures, they are eager to please, they love their master, and are inherently loyal. However, if you choose to let them grow up in your life without discipline, they, like any other dog, will become wild and mean. Should you choose not to put well disciplined puppies into your life which will let them grow to mature, loving, and loyal creatures, LET ME ASSURE YOU, YOU WILL CONTINUE TO LIVE A DOG'S LIFE, FINANCIALLY.

PEACE PUPPIES

1) Avoid "Stuffitis"-The Worship of "Stuff"
2) Plant Seeds-Give Money Away To Worthy Causes

CHAPTER FIVE

BUYER BEWARE
(CAVEAT EMPTOR)

In the 1970's when I started in the real estate business there was a saying taught us in Latin. "Caveat Emptor", which means "let the buyer beware." The context in which we were taught it was residential real estate where the seller of the property normally pays the real estate commission. Since the seller is paying the agents, the buyer technically has no representation so he should "beware." In this age of governmental bureaucracy we assume that there is always someone or some agency watching out for us as consumers. We take that for granted. In truth, we are fairly sheltered from actual scams and/or dangerous products.

WE WANT YOUR MONEY

However, we are ignorant as to how much effort, time, energy, and MONEY is spent to get our business and thereby our money. While companies spend billions of dollars and hours to sell to us, we sit idly by getting sold and sold and sold. If you are to ever get control of your financial life you must learn to "Just say NO" to buying. Most families buy themselves into financial ruin.

POWER OVER PURCHASE

We must develop a:

POWER OVER PURCHASE

instead of all our purchases and the people from which we make the purchases having power over us. We must remember that you can ALWAYS spend more than you can make. I met a man whose income went from $42,000 annually to $175,000 annually in one year. Both years he spent everything he made. He had no sales resistance, no power over purchase.

Proverbs 14:29 says "He who is impulsive exalts folly."

PROFILE OF THE ENEMY

For me to label every honest company or person who wants to sell you something, "the enemy," may seem overstated, but they can be the enemy of your financial peace of mind. It is time the American consumer quit being so lazy in the purchase decisions he makes. We are sold goods and services by what are many times juvenile tactics and strategies just because of our laziness.

First, the subject of personal selling: Where the item is sold to you by a person one-on-one and there is discussion. This can be as insignificant as, "Do you want fries with you food order, Sir?" Just by adding that statement to every whopper flopper's training, the gross sales of those companies go up millions of dollars annually.

However, the personal selling we are most concerned with involves larger ticket items. The sale of cars, houses, financial products, furniture, electronics, etc. etc. Any company that is going to survive in today's business climate selling any of these items has HIGHLY trained professional salespeople. Sometimes these salespeople are trained to spout certain pat lines, but even these pat lines are highly developed by upper management. Millions of dollars are spent by companies each year teaching their front-line people how to dress, talk, and walk in order to influence you to buy. A car salesperson who doesn't have five answers to " I want to think about it" will soon starve. A stereo salesperson who lets you off the property without a sale knows over 90% of the time he has lost that sale. A real estate agent who doesn't make it easy to look past the bright red bedroom and help you through the rigors of finance won't make it. I have sold many a kitchen to a woman and the house just went with it or sold a big basement to a man and the house just went with it. Good salespeople know a customer who asks a question about the product or service is giving what is called "a buying signal," so the salesperson will just turn on the pitch that much more. For example, a good car salesman will not just answer yes or no to a question like "Do you have that car in stock in blue?" Instead he will answer you with "If we do, would you rather finance that on 48 or 60 months" and when you answer that question you are that much closer to buying that car.

This is not a game! It is how these people make a living and if they are not good at persuading you to spend your money on their product or service they simply starve out of the business, so the sale is very, very important to them. The sale is also important to their company who by assisting them in selling will also stand to profit. I am not saying that we go into a hypnotic state in which we lose all will-power just because a good salesperson is on the scene, I am saying WAKE UP! They are there and they do have a substantial impact on your decision of whether or not to purchase, especially, if you are unaware and/or are just being mentally lazy.

NOTHING DOWN, NOTHING A MONTH

Another way products and services are sold to you is by offering you unbelievable financing. Have you ever heard of "ninety days same as cash," or "no finance charges until January," or "no interest financing?" Did it ever occur to you that in a world so driven by money markets that a company offering zero interest with no ulterior motive would soon go broke?

Here is how it really works. First, the product is priced higher to cover the expense, so there is actually no savings, but the story just starts there. Most dealers in this type of approach use a finance company to buy the contract once you execute it. Why would a finance company buy a contract at zero interest? Two reasons, first the dealer (the furniture or stereo store, etc.) who marked up the item anyway sells the financing contract to the finance company at a discount. The dealer got what he wanted, a sale and at a normal profit after the discount to the finance company.

So when you come in on the 89th day of 90 days same as cash and pay off the finance company they make a profit.

More importantly though one of my friends who is a regional manager for a nationally known finance company tells me that over 70% of the time YOU DO NOT PAY HIM OFF inside the stated period. The finance company gladly begins to charge you interest and puts you on a longer pay plan. That is okay except normally when this occurs you are paying over 24% interest (if your state allows it) and the contract is on prepaid interest or "rule of 78s" which means you have a huge pre-payment penalty. They also normally will sell you overpriced life and disability insurance to pay off their overpriced loan should something happen to your overpriced self.

You are in good company, I know a financial planner who bought his VCR this way and even he ended up converting to *easy* payments. Your brilliant zero interest plan now has turned into one of the worst financial decisions you ever made because of the total cost of that item. A $1,000 couch at 24% for 3 years with life and disability will end up costing you at least $1900. Be aware of financing as a method of selling. Learn not to just ask, "How much down and how much a month?" Until you learn this lesson you will never have financial peace.

I LOVE TV, (JUST KIDDING)

Also, beware of the subtle sales methods advertisers use on you and your children. Television and radio advertisers understand the power of repetition. Most well-known products are well-known because companies spend millions on "brand recognition" positioning their product in your mind as better because of brand. Physiological studies are done to measure your body's reaction to color, label design, and shelf position. The astute company knows what your heart rate, retina reaction, pupil dilation, peripheral vision, protein release, adrenalin release, and many other reactions are to their products and/or its packaging or shelf position. A nationally known real estate franchise at its inception spent over $250,000 studying and developing the color to use on it's yard signs just to make sure your eye would be more likely to notice that house for sale.

I recently sat in on an upper management meeting for a nationally known restaurant where they spent hours discussing minute details like the positioning of tables and/or hostess stations to make patrons feel more comfortable, but at the same time create more "table turns" meaning eating faster so tables are open for other paying customers.

A cold drink man will fight like mad for the best shelf position in a convenience mart. I have even heard of a bread man or candy man or cigarette man that would physically sabotage or fight for a certain position for a display. This may seem silly or minor to you. However, these companies have learned years ago that proper display or shelf positioning will control *your* impulse buying decisions and therefore their sales may go up or down 500% simply by poor vs. good positioning. This is not a game to them!! Companies are thinking about and implementing detailed strategies, and you must build some defenses against them or you will never get control of your finances.

Lastly, be aware that your body reacts chemically when you make a "significant purchase." Companies understand from documented research the chemical changes a buyer experiences when making a purchase that is "significant" in terms of its cost. A "significant" purchase is not a candy bar. For most people it is something over $300. As you move through the stages of making a buying decision your heart rate increases, your pupils dilate, and your body releases adrenaline, proteins, hormones, and enzymes. In short no matter how low key you are on the outside you are getting excited. Any of these changes stated above in excess could be attributed to a drug addict on a high. Buyers do get a small "rush" from making these purchases. The people selling you call it "the fever" or "buying fever." They know it exists and that you are partially influenced by it. Now you know too, so beware.

THE BIG TICKET

Several years ago I sold new homes on a building site that sold for $150,000 and up per home. In selling these properties we were aware of this "rush" phenomenon. The average couple who would make a purchase, and sign a contract would roll over the next morning and look at each other with fear in their eyes and a knot in their stomachs and say, "what in the world have we done?" We called this "buyer's remorse" and everyone who has lived very long has experienced it. As sales people we learned to counteract their wanting out of the deal the next day by telling them in great detail that this "buyer's remorse" was going to happen to them and if it didn't they were not normal. So when Joe and Sue would roll over the next morning after our explanation with fear in their hearts, they would just sigh with relief because they were normal. This technique avoided a lot of contract cancellations. Be aware of yourself when making a "significant" purchase.

What to do? You are NOT helpless. So quit acting like it. You just need to be aware of the other side of this coin. When making your purchases you should first:

carefully consider your buying motives.

Why do you want or think you need this item? Could you live without it? Do you want it for selfish reasons like showing up the neighbors, or does the item have utility to you?

Next, *SLOW DOWN!!* You need to make purchases slower and you will make better decisions. If the purchase is a "significant purchase" never buy it without waiting overnight. Sounds old fashioned, not very '90's advice. Well so be it, the people of past generations didn't make the bad buying decisions we have made. They didn't have record foreclosures and bankruptcies which are the norm of today.

Proverbs 14:29 says "He who is impulsive exalts folly."

Lastly, you should seek counsel and look carefully for bargains and I have devoted entire chapters to these two ideas.

Remember you must develop :

POWER OVER PURCHASE

rather than letting the purchases continue having power over you. The definition of a rich man: a person who is not AFRAID to ask to see something cheaper.

PEACE PUPPIES

1) Avoid "Stuffitis"-The Worship of "Stuff"
2) Plant Seeds-Give Money Away To Worthy Causes
3) Develop Your Own "Power Over Purchase"

CHAPTER SIX

CAREER CHOICE

The career or type of work you choose and whether or not you choose to *work* at it can be paramount to your financial peace.

Douglas MacGregor said, "Man is a wanting animal-as soon as one of his needs is satisfied, another appears in its place. This process is unending. It continues from birth to death. Man continuously puts forth effort-works, if you please-to satisfy his needs."

THAT MAKES ME TIRED

We spend well in excess of 100,000 hours working at our choice vocation in our lives. The sheer math of a per hour rate makes this decision very important. You must plan your work and then work your plan. Happy and effective people are those who have found a vocation that they have a natural aptitude for and then have gone about doing that vocation extremely well. These are the people who have a vacation for a vocation.

DO WHAT COMES NATURALLY

You have a natural talent or aptitude in some area or areas. Not only does it make you happier to function and successfully perform in that role, but you will sooner or later become very well paid for that. Our free market system cannot help but pay for performance at some point. When you have a natural talent or aptitude and you couple that with desire and experience, the result is productivity plus. This concept is so important to you financially that I recommend if you are not happy and functioning at peak efficiency, you should immediately find an aptitude testing center and be tested. I am talking about a detailed test. These tests are sometimes expensive, but in relative terms if you find you have an aptitude for an industry where your pay would go to $75,000 to $100,000 within just a few years and you are making $30,000 now at a job you hate, that is a good deal. The economic change will easily make the testing pay its way, not to mention the self growth in terms of "know thyself" that occurs.

GO FORTH

Should you find or think that you are currently where you should be, IT IS TIME TO EXCEL. Get off your backside and do the work necessary to excel in what you do. There is a rule in business that says if you are going to eat, and eat excellently, you must get up, leave the cave, go and kill something and drag it home. The boss can't do it for you, the company can't do it for you, and the competition can't do it *to* you if you have made up your mind to succeed.

I am not talking about some hyped-up vision of success, just hard hard work at something you are naturally good at which will sooner or later catapult you to where you want to be. In most industries you can simply out-work 80% of your cohorts and out-smart (knowledge) 15% of the rest, putting you in the top 5% which always pays very well.

THE TWO CYCLES

You see, if you are good at something, it normally makes you more intense so you get more creative. Consequently you accomplish more so you get paid more. Whereby you enjoy it more which then, in turn, means you will get better at it. This becomes what we call an excellence cycle. If you get caught up in a excellence cycle, you will find your financial problems will no longer be caused by a low income.

On the other hand you can, and many do, get caught in a death cycle. When you came out of school you may have given as much thought to your career as what clothes to put on that day, so you entered a field not well suited for you. Some of you did give extensive thought to your direction or your parents or friends gave thought to YOUR direction and that may have had the same disastrous effect. If so, you hate what you do, so you are less intense so you are less creative. As a result you accomplish less, so you get paid less or level off. So you become even more unhappy, which then starts the cycle again. Get out!!

Start making plans today to get away from your bad situation as soon as you can. Get tested and then get in a field you should be in and will enjoy. You will be happier, healthier, and wealthier. However, DO NOT QUIT TODAY!! Do not get all excited and destroy your monthly budget by making a rash decision. I am saying do BEGIN the process of discovery and transformation TODAY.

Sometimes it is financially necessary that you take an extra job for the income needed just to provide the basics. Second jobs are a hard thing to do but can make a career transition smoother from the financial perspective. Do what you have to do in the short term to make the long term happen.

THE SECOND INCOME OR IS IT?

Many families today have found it necessary to have two incomes to exist. Many women do very well in careers and find much satisfaction. However, in counseling couples, many times I find a wife and mother working at something she hates because the bills and her husband require that she "do her part."

In many cases this can be an economic myth. Note this example of one of my clients, a working mom with two kids making a pretty good income. Or is she?

Working Mom $18,000 Annual Salary

MONTHLY	YEARLY	
1,500	18,000	Income
		minus:
550	6,600	Taxes and pay roll deduction
950	11,400	Take home pay
		minus:
100	1,200	More extensive wardrobe
45	540	Extra dry cleaning
50	600	Extra mileage depreciates car
50	600	Extra maintenance on car
560	6,720	Day care 2 kids $65 each per wk
50	600	Extra meals out due to fatigue
95	1,140	Real Net Income

This is not to say that women should not work. If a woman is productive and enjoys what she does, then by all means she should go for it. But, ladies, do not let the "me generation" trap you into thinking the only way to have a reasonable style of living is to work your fingers to the bone, because all you may be getting is *bony fingers*.

Don't let the "me generation" trick you into thinking the only method for people to be all they can be is in the work place. Many highly intelligent, articulate, employable women choose a career in the home and they should not be shamed for doing so. The so called politically correct thing to do may not be. Even what may on the surface appear to be the economically correct thing to do with some serious inquiry does not prove out.

GET REAL, GET FOCUSED

When you find the right field of endeavor for you, you will excel financially only if you work hard and are honest. The same light widely disbursed in a room simply lights the room, but when focused to the size of a pin becomes a laser. You must do some self inspection at this point to determine if you are lazy. That is harsh, but I have never met a lazy person who thinks he is lazy.

If you are taking extra time off and calling it sick days when you are not sick, if you are working half speed when the supervisor is not watching, you are guilty of theft. You are stealing from the company which supports your family, but worst of all you are making a statement about who you are.

It is time we turned the corner on this issue of low productivity. Sadly, in most cases, low productivity is people simply not working hard. When we are managing people, or when we are being managed, we must do everything we can to maximize our time. When we "be all we can be" the result will eventually be a pay raise, maybe not how you think, but it will.

THE PROOF, NEED I SAY MORE?

I had an administrative assistant working for me once who was wonderful. She was great with people, had a natural aptitude for watching the books, handled the telephone very well, and had a myriad of secretarial skills. When I lost everything I had to let her go. I had no trouble placing her in a better paying job. Not only did she get a raise leaving me, she has since moved up through that company like a rocket, so she got a much better position than I was giving her. Everyone that had contact with my company was impressed with her positive outlook and ability to get things done, so I just had to make about five phone calls, and she got a better job when leaving us. She never did the things she did for my company in order to get that job later, she simply did what was asked and a little more, every time. That is true of any position in any field, so work hard, you never know who is watching!!

Matthew 7:12 "Therefore whatever you want men to do to you, do also to them..."

Career Choice

During a period of economic hardship due to high interest rates in the real estate business, my mother sent me the following poem in the mail, and it hangs on my office wall today.

THE ROOSTER AND THE HEN

Said the Little Red Rooster,
"Believe me things are tough!
Seems the worms are getting scarcer
And I cannot find enough.
What's become of all those fat ones?
It's a mystery to me.
There were thousands through that rainy spell,
But now, where can they be?"

But the Old Black Hen who heard him
didn't grumble or complain,
She had lived through lots of dry spells
She had lived through floods of rain.
She picked a new and undug spot,
The ground was hard and firm,
"I must go to the worms," she said.
"The worms won't come to me."

The Rooster vainly spent his day
Through habit, by the ways
Where fat round worms had passed in squads
Back in the rainy days.
When nightfall found him supperless,
He growled in accents rough,
"I'm hungry as a fowl can be,
Conditions sure are tough."

But the Old Black Hen hopped to her perch
And dropped her eyes to sleep
And murmured in a drowsy tone,
"Young man, hear this and weep.
I'm full of worms and happy
For I've eaten like a pig.
The worms were there as always
But, boy I had to dig!"

This was a Depression Era Poem, Strange it still applies today, Love Mom

PEACE PUPPIES

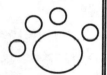

1) Avoid "Stuffitis"-The Worship of "Stuff"
2) Plant Seeds-Give Money Away To Worthy Causes
3) Develop Your Own "Power Over Purchase"
4) Find What You Are Naturally Gifted At, Enjoy Your
     Work, And Work Hard

CHAPTER SEVEN

LIFESTYLES OF THE RICH

Avoid the lifestyles of the rich WHEN YOU ARE NOT RICH. I have learned that the best things in life including good *"stuff"* come only at the expense of personal discipline. Many of my suggestions may not appear "fun" in the short run, but in actuality are a lot more "fun" in the long run.

"Almost any man knows how to earn money, but not one in a million knows how to spend it."
                                        - Henry David Thoreau

NO WAY AROUND IT

You must limit your style of living. You must figure out what your actual income is and then proceed to live far below that mark. You may respond "That is impossible!!!"   No, it is not impossible. It will take some time to undo some of the messes you have gotten yourself into (and we will help you), but it is very possible.

Experts have written about and tracked the baby boomer's financial growth and spending habits for years. What they have all found is while most couples get married broke, within three or four years they have attempted to copy their parents net worth and lifestyle. Again, Larry Burkett says that usually because of the broad spectrum of borrowing available to them they can achieve almost the same lifestyle that it took their parents 25 years to achieve. These couples drive the same cars, live only blocks away, except in a new house and have nicer clothes than their parents, who make more money and have worked a lifetime to attain these possessions. The only problem is the new couple has covered themselves in every imaginable type of debt so their financial ship is very unsteady. Why? Because they could not say no to themselves.

HERE IS HOW IT STARTS

The normal scenario goes like this: Joe and Sue get married and have no assets. I mean they are B-R-O-K-E. You remember, "Honey, we don't need money we got love," and a good thing too because they are eating off a card table and driving a 15-year-old Pinto. Many of us started house-keeping this way, but expanded quickly. That neat new job had a neat new pay check that went with it, and we had to find something to do with all that money. So Joe and Sue began to buy *"stuff"* and finance most of the purchases. The new cars had notes, the stereo, the waterbed, and now that new house all have payments. Lets look in on Joe and Sue after 3 to 5 years of marriage.

Income Monthly		**3,500**
minus:		
House Payment	875	
Equity Line	120	
Car Payment *	310	
Miscellaneous	115	
Utilities	430	
Gas Card	85	
Master Card	120	
VISA	95	
Food	600	
Car Repair	75	
Clothes	100	
Car Insurance	120	
Life Insurance	75	
Car Gasoline	180	
Net Disposable Income		**200**
*(old car is paid for)		

This is a typical budget for a middle class couple, and if these numbers hit close to home, it is because I've seen hundreds of these situations. Some items will vary from region to region, but we will use these numbers for our discussion.

So Joe and Sue have $3,500 coming in and $3,300 going out, and this budget does not account for many other things. This is a disaster looking for a place to happen, as we will see later. Let's continue, Joe makes $2,400 per month gross, and he comes home one day all excited because he has gotten a 10% raise, and he is particularly excited because things have been awfully tight lately.

DO WE SLOW DOWN, OF COURSE NOT

However, there is the matter of that old car Sue reminds him, it does seem to break down a lot. They decide they need to go car shopping, and they promptly fall in love with this wonderful new bright red car, and, after all, the dealer did give them a great trade-in on that old clunker. I heard a man say once that the worst car accidents happen on the showroom floor. So here is what they buy:

$16,000 car financed over 7 years at 14% with payments of $300 per month. Value of car after 7 years is about $800.

So Joe and Sue got a raise of $200 per month and then promptly go and commit to an additional payment of $300 per month. This process is unfortunately the normal one and they now have income of $3,700 and outflow of $3,600, very tight. That is the normal approach, but if they were going to commit to spend $300 per month they could have done this:

$5,400 car financed over 7 years at 14% is payments of $100 per month. Value of car after 7 years is about $400 The other $200 per month saved at 10% for 7 years is going to grow to $24,190.
NOW WHO MADE THE CORRECT CHOICE !!!!!

WHOA BOY!!

Slow down!! You must evaluate carefully your purchase decisions because, as you see, if you will sacrifice for a few years, you can live easier later. By strapping ourselves to all these lifestyle purchases to live well we actually cause an ongoing cancer that will prevent us from ever living well.

While we are in pursuit of this elusive brass ring, we often get involved with some sort of get-rich-quick approaches to business. Beware! If you limit your lifestyle you can avoid this pit fall because you will be focusing on long range security.

In a book called "Money Talks," Bob Edwards is quoted as saying, "If one-half of a man's schemes turned out according to his preliminary figures, he would have nothing to do but spend his money."

Within the first couple of years after college I bought dinner for several very wealthy people in order to pick those successful brains. One gentleman in his 70's who had acquired much wealth over his lifetime as a shopping center developer was nice enough to allow that aggressive young man to buy his dinner.

After about an hour of my asking, digging, and searching him for answers of how I might duplicate his success he finally looked me square in the eye across the table and said "Boy, seems to me you want to know how to get rich quick." To which I replied "Of course." So he paused a long time to add suspense and then said "The best way to get rich quick is to NOT get rich quick." Now, years later, I have often thought of that man and his very wise advice as I sit and cry with some couple that have tried so hard to live like the wealthy when they weren't and set themselves up for financial disaster.

YOU CAN ALWAYS SPEND IT

You must limit your style of living, because you can always spend more than you can make. I have counseled people who make $200,000 annually, and people who make $20,000, and they both spent it all. Yes, the guy with $200,000 had bigger toys and more sophisticated bad investments, but they both had the same broke result. B-R-O-K-E

Having been in business several years in Nashville, Tennessee (Music City, USA) I have had the pleasure of seeing some fortunes made in the music business. A personal friend was a writer for one of the very well-known country music groups a few years back. One day he called, all excited, to say he had gotten two songs he had co-written on this group's latest album. I thought, "So what?". No big deal just half-writer royalties on two songs that don't go single is nothing huge.

THE BIG TIME

This gentleman went from $700 per month to over $50,000 per month for four or five months. He proceeded to do what any red blooded American would do. He began to buy *"stuff"*, LOTS OF *"STUFF"*. On Thursday he pulled up in front of our home to show us his $40,000 black convertible sports car. Then his friend pulled in behind him. They had bought matching black convertibles and paid full sticker price. On Saturday he pulled up with a new dual-wheel truck loaded with options and attached to the back of it was a 36' mini yacht. He had bought the boat and didn't have a way to pull it so he bought the truck. A few months later, of course, the checks stopped as the album peaked and died, but the payments he had obligated for didn't stop. Today he is bankrupt and writing songs for $700 per month again.

NOT ME, NEVER ME

You say, " that will never happen to me", but I bet it already has only in a smaller fashion. Remember what Joe and Sue did with their raise? The same thing my friend did. Both parties immediately raised their standard of living to keep right up with the income increases. Why not try to keep the same style of living? I know it is tempting to treat yourself, I have done it but I have learned you are sacrificing the future when you do.

Most of our society defines a financial genius as someone who can make money faster than he can spend it. We are beginning to learn differently. At age 26 I owned over 4 million dollars worth of real estate and I thought I was hot *"stuff"*. I was so cool that I didn't want to be seen in possession of anything that wasn't considered expensive, so I threw away an old leather briefcase that was functional and purchased a very expensive leather case. The latches on this expensive case broke within 6 months. About that time I was beginning to get a handle on some of these principles of money so I made myself carry that "expensive" case with no latches under my arm for 2 years to remind myself that more expensive isn't always better.

WHAT DOES IT MATTER?

Often when I am teaching before a crowd I show my watch which is a brand name no one has ever heard of. I tell them this watch is the latest fad, the very best quality known to man to date, and all the millionaires want one, but they are hard to find. I will even take the watch off and let someone hold it while telling them it cost over $6,000. After everyone is sufficiently impressed, I will tell them the truth, which is, all those statements are lies. The watch was purchased at a discount department store for $19.95 on sale. I know you think that you would never fall for that, but this particular watch is reasonably attractive, and most people believe me. I use this example to illustrate the ridiculous purchases we sometimes make. Whether that watch cost $6,000 or $20 is irrelevant to anyone but my family because it tells time and is acceptably attractive. It is only relevant to my family because of what it did to or for my household budget.

You see we have gradually slipped. So gradually that many of us did what we would never intellectually admit to doing . . . We let some yuppie client or neighbor influence what we thought was important. "Please don't say it!" I have to. We started acting as if we really did need to keep up with the Jones. "Oh no, not me" you say. I challenge you to look *not* at your thoughts, but at the major purchases you have made during the last 3 years and the motivations behind those purchases. That is the acid test.

THIS IS HOW THE REAL RICH DO IT

Many wealthy people I meet really do live only upper middle class lifestyles. Many extremely wealthy people I know, who have had wealth for many years, live lower middle class lifestyles and don't suffer in the least. They understood a limited lifestyle is what got them there, and they forgot to increase their lifestyle even to what most people call tolerable conditions.

I once met with a man worth over 10 million dollars and his office was furnished with black rotary phones, and in his "reception area," if you would call it that, there was a vinyl couch with cuts in the cushions from the springs coming through. I am not suggesting you dip to the poverty level, but it is interesting how people live who have wealth.

Proverbs 21:20 says "In the house of the wise are stores of choice food and oil, BUT A FOOLISH MAN DEVOURS ALL HE HAS."

PEACE PUPPIES

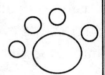

1) Avoid "Stuffitis"-The Worship of "Stuff"
2) Plant Seeds-Give Money Away To Worthy Causes
3) Develop Your Own "Power Over Purchase"
4) Find What You Are Naturally Gifted At, Enjoy Your
          Work, And Work Hard
5) Live Substantially Below Your Income
6) Sacrifice Now So You Can Have Peace Later
7) You Can Always Spend More Than You Can Make

CHAPTER EIGHT

PILE UP PLUNDER

Pile up plunder, save money, SAVE MONEY, S-a-v-e M-o-n-e-y, you must save money. I do not know how to say it any more plainly. You must save some of what you make out of every check, or you will never acquire any peace in your finances. This is a very elementary principle, but NO ONE DOES IT. Many financial geniuses will be sitting there reading this book with their nose in the air saying "This writer sure is basic" or "Can't he be any more original than that?", but even they don't save money. We live in one of the richest countries in the world, and the average family does not have over $1,000 in the bank. The actual statistics are that we as a people save less than 3% of our annual income.

ONLY YOU CAN PREVENT FOREST FIRES

Tax incentives can't help you save. Spouses that badger can't help. Employer savings programs can help, but only you and a change in your discipline can cause savings to occur. I will spend the balance of this chapter trying to give you reasons to save, but until you resolve to save, and are willing to give up something now so that you might have more peace later, savings will not occur. I feel that you should have a goal of saving 10% of your take home pay. You work and slave at that job to bring home the bacon. Then what happens? Your checkbook simply serves as a clearing account for the people you owe and the *"stuff"* you buy. The money goes in and ALL the money goes out instantly. Only the names were changed to protect the innocent. I know, because I did it that way for years too. If you work that hard, and most of you do, then it is time to put a new name on your list of bills.

PAY ME, PLEASE PAY ME

At the top of the list every week write first the money you will give away. The very next line should be "PAY ME" and then make sure those bills are paid. It is ridiculous for you to spend your entire life at your given occupation only to end up broke and discouraged because you did not write "PAY ME" at the top of the page.

There are many programs to help you save called "forced savings plans." Most of you need to use something that helps you have discipline to save. If you have access to a credit union, they will set up a payroll deduction savings plan. The savings is deducted before you get your check, that way you don't have a chance to do anything else with it. Most of your local banks also have forced saving programs to help you force yourself to save. If you need to start this way, DO IT.

PAC MAN

Many insurance companies and security brokerage firms use a PAC (Pre-Authorized Checking) withdrawal system. On a certain day each month a stated amount is automatically withdrawn from your checking account and deposited into the savings program of your choice. These savings programs are annuities, money markets, mutual funds, etc. and can be very good. However, you must take the time to understand what you are putting your money into or you can get stung by some of these programs. I do not recommend a life insurance policy as a place to build up savings or cash value. BEWARE. We will discuss these policies further in a later chapter.

The most effective way to save is by applying discipline over a period of time, as opposed to trying to save in big splashes. I feel there are at least two main reasons to save money. First, you should save until you have built an emergency fund, and second, you should save for wealth building.

EMERGENCY FUND

If you are a big income earner of $150,000 plus per year, you and many people like you may have gone to a big time "financial planner" and paid him a fee of $2,000 or more per year to "advise" you on your financial plans. Most people do not make that kind of income, but we should learn from what these big income earners are taught.

A good financial planner will tell you that FIRST you should have three to six months of income in savings that are liquid just for emergencies. Liquid means you need to have that three to six months of income saved and stored where you can get it very quickly and easily. An example is a simple bank savings account or a money market fund that has check writing capability. A Certificate of Deposit that has a big interest penalty for early withdrawal is not very liquid nor is an investment in rental real estate.

If you make $36,000 you should have $9,000 to $18,000 where you can easily get it BEFORE you do ANY other investing. I know that seems like a lot of money especially when most only have $1,000 in the bank now, but here is why the experts tell us we should save so much.

SINGING IN THE RAIN

Do you remember your grandmother telling you to save for a "rainy day." She was right. It will rain and why not be in a position to cover the problem and be caught "singing in the rain" rather than crying.

Never has a couple come to me for crisis financial counseling that had an emergency fund of three to six months income. Remember Joe and Sue? After they bought that second car for $300 per month their budget had $3,700 income and $3,600 outflow, I said that was a disaster looking for a place to happen. Because people are normally cruising along at "tight" level when the devastating "UNEXPECTED EVENT" occurs. Sue gets pregnant, or Joe gets laid off, or Joe gets hurt on the job (temporary disability 70% of pay), or there is a death in the family and they must share the expense, or one of the wonderful cars has a major breakdown, or a child has an accident requiring major medical, or or or . . .

OF BOATS AND TORPEDOS

Joe and Sue's financial boat is cruising along already loaded to the brim and they get this $3,000 to $10,000 torpedo in the form of an "UNEXPECTED EVENT." Then they are sinking fast and they start to play "juggle the bills." You know the game - you decide who *doesn't* get paid this month. Too much month left at the end of the money. By the time they get to my office they have so many balls, er, I mean bills, in the air they are out of control. If they only had an emergency fund to cushion the blow from the "UNEXPECTED EVENT" torpedo.

A SIMPLE TEST

Lay this book down now. Hold your right hand up in front of you with your elbow bent, now reach your left hand across the back of your wrist to where your finger tips touch your main artery and then check for pulse. Is your heart beating? Then in actuality there are no "UNEXPECTED EVENTS" financially. If you are alive and walking around things WILL happen to you that you don't think will. The only way you can avoid unexpected financial events is not to be alive, so they are NOT "unexpected" events, are they?

I am simply telling you that you must plan for the unexpected, because it will happen. Although we don't know what form it will take; it will come; cars do break; women do get pregnant; people do die and get hurt; businesses do lay people off; and to think otherwise is naive. So plan for it Buckwheat. Otay? Saving into an emergency fund first is an essential element for financial peace.

WHAT IS A BODY TO DO?

Should I pay off my credit cards or debts before saving into an emergency fund? Both. I mean you should begin a balanced plan of saving and debt reduction. Even if it is only $25 in saving and $25 in extra payments to reduce debt, do something positive. You need to see the positive results of both happening, not one then the other. Please note that with no savings and credit card debt there is no doubt your credit cards have been your emergency fund. That is very bad planning that will spiral you downward and that habit pattern will likely land you in bankruptcy, if left unchecked.

SAVING FOR WEALTH

Remember the "Money is Active" principle. Here is where you can see just how active. Most consumers do not understand how quickly time, interest rates, and payments, work for them or against them. At work in your money is a mathematical monster called compound interest. Compound interest is either financially your best friend if you make him work for you, or your worst possible enemy if he works against you. If you are saving at good interest rates, and you do so every month, and are doing so for many years compound interest is your best friend, However, if you have borrowed over long periods of time at high interest rates you see him as your worst enemy. Mathematically speaking compound interest works exponentially or in a geometric progression. In English, this simply means that your money is affected by a mathematical multiplied explosion, not by simply $1+1=2$.

Get out the payment schedule on your house or your car and look at how the first bunch of payments are almost all interest and how you have paid back almost no debt. That is compound interest working against you, but it can work just as strongly for you.

WATCH CLOSELY NOW

Let me show you what I mean. If you start to save at age 25 with the idea that you will withdraw your money at age 65 you will save 40 years. Let's say that you put $1,000 in a savings account one time at age 25 and you never deposited or withdrew anything from that account (you just let the interest compound or grow) until age 65.

THE REAL NUMBERS

At 6% per year you would have just over $10,000 at age 65, so if we double the interest rate to 12% you should have around $16,000 right? WRONG!!! You will have just over $93,000 at 12% at age 65. That is compound interest working for you and you see the multiplication effect rather that the addition effect that most may have thought. But, let's raise the rate of interest again to 18% (which many good solid mutual funds have)(Danger: use mutual funds only for long term investments). So at 18% what will we have? $750,378 !!!

$1,000 one time investment, no withdrawal
Age 25 to Age 65 (40 years)

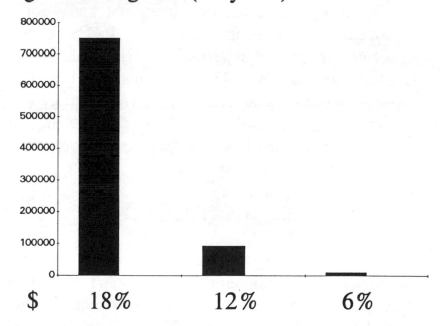

18% = $750,378
12% = $ 93,050
 6% = $ 10,285

Are you beginning to understand that the rate and term at which you save or borrow is very important? Now let me show you how banks make a profit. Do you have a bank credit card? Do you have a savings account with that bank? Many people are loaning the bank their money in a savings account at 6% or less and then borrowing their own money back by having a credit card balance and paying 18%. If you left $1,000 in a savings account like this, and kept a $1,000 balance on your credit card, the bank will have made the spread at virtually no risk and with no investment for a $740,093 profit for every time this happens in our 40-year example. If you multiply this scenario times thousands of customers it is enough to make you understand how the banks own most of the tall buildings in every major city.

A LITTLE BIT GOES A LONG WAY

To further show you how important the understanding of compound interest is and it's power in your finances, let's look at retirement. If you started at age 25, and saved for 40 years until age 65, saving only $60 per month (but EVERY month) at 14% average annual return (which a long term growth mutual fund could easily do.) You would accumulate $1,341,263.00 to retire on. There is no excuse why everyone, if he acquires this knowledge early enough, should not retire a millionaire. Compound interest is powerful, and remember it works for, or against you with equal power.

WOW WHAT A CAR

Remember Joe and Sue? Let's pick on them some more. Remember they bought a $16,000 car for $300 per month. I said they should have held back and bought a $5,400 car for $100 per month and saved the other $200 per month at 10% for seven years, giving them $24,190 at the end. As long as they stay on the first plan they will have car payments the rest of their lives, compound interest working against them. However using my Plan II let's carry the scenario years into the future. At year seven the car is junk, in either plan, but let's say that they saved that $24,190 and they went out and bought a $16,000 car for cash from that savings, leaving them $8,190.

THE NEW CAR

They now have a new car with no car payment and $8,190 in the bank, but let's go yet another seven years. They have no car payment so instead of the $100 payment and the $200 savings they were doing every month, now they decide just to save $100 per month freeing up $200 per month. At the end of seven more years that $8,190 left over, plus $100 per month, plus 10% interest will grow to

$28,539. Now they again have a seven year old car that is worthless, so they buy yet another $16,000 car for cash leaving $12,539 in savings. For yet the next seven years they have no car payment and, though *they do no additional savings* the $12,539 at 10% will grow to $24,436!

PAY ME NOW OR PAY ME BIG LATER

That is a hard chain of events to follow. The bottom line is if Joe and Sue would sacrifice for a lesser purchase up front and save the difference, then continue that process they will be driving "paid for" cars and have savings the rest of their lives. That is compound interest working for you. Again, the best way to get rich quick is to NOT get rich quick, but watch your decisions, and time will make you wealthy.

This idea, to save a certain monthly amount with interest in order to have the amount needed to make your purchases, is called "a sinking fund." The concept of a sinking fund is simple. It is making payments in reverse. If you want $4,000 for a dinning room suite. Instead of borrowing it at 24% why don't you use a sinking fund savings program. Save $151 per month for 24 months at 10%, and then pay cash. Note: 151 X 24 is only $3,624, the rest is interest in your favor. But if you financed it at 24% at the furniture store you would have paid $151 for 31 months and will have paid $4,681 for the same suite, not to mention the discount you should get for flashing cash (to be covered later). All you need to design a sinking fund for any purchase is a simple financial calculator, or your banker can probably help you figure out your program especially if you are saving in his bank. Always remember to make the power of compound interest work FOR you.

BERT OR ERNIE, WHO IS THE SMARTER?

Bernard Zick, a MBA (Masters in Business Administration), and an expert in the time value of money gave this consumer quiz in his monthly newsletter:

Ben, age 22, invests $1,000 per year compounded annually at 10% for 8 years until he is 30 years old. For the next 35 years, until he is 65, Ben invests not one penny more.

Arthur, age 30, invests $1,000 per year for 35 years until he is 65 years old. His investment also earns 10% compound interest per year. At age 65, will Arthur or Ben have the most money?

The answer diagramed on the next page is yet another example strongly showing you must understand the power of compound interest and get started NOW !!!

Pile up Plunder

AGE	BEN INVESTS		ARTHUR INVESTS	
22	1,000	1,100	0	0
23	1,000	2,310	0	0
24	1,000	3,641	0	0
25	1,000	5,105	0	0
26	1,000	6,716	0	0
27	1,000	8,487	0	0
28	1,000	10,436	0	0
29	1,000	12,579	0	0
30	0	13,837	1,000	1,100
31	0	15,221	1,000	2,310
32	0	16,743	1,000	3,641
33	0	18,418	1,000	5,105
34	0	20,259	1,000	6,716
35	0	22,285	1,000	8,487
36	0	24,514	1,000	10,436
37	0	26,965	1,000	12,579
38	0	29,662	1,000	14,937
39	0	32,628	1,000	17,531
40	0	35,891	1,000	20,384
41	0	39,480	1,000	23,523
42	0	43,428	1,000	26,975
43	0	47,771	1,000	30,772
44	0	52,548	1,000	34,950
45	0	57,802	1,000	39,545
46	0	63,583	1,000	44,599
47	0	69,941	1,000	50,159
48	0	76,935	1,000	56,275
49	0	84,628	1,000	63,002
50	0	93,091	1,000	70,403
51	0	102,400	1,000	78,543
52	0	112,640	1,000	87,497
53	0	123,904	1,000	97,347
54	0	136,295	1,000	108,182
55	0	149,924	1,000	120,100
56	0	164,917	1,000	133,210
57	0	181,409	1,000	147,631
58	0	199,549	1,000	163,494
59	0	219,504	1,000	180,943
60	0	241,455	1,000	200,138
61	0	265,600	1,000	221,252
62	0	292,160	1,000	244,477
63	0	321,376	1,000	270,024
64	0	353,514	1,000	298,127
65	**0**	**388,865**	**1,000**	**329,039**

..... *AND HE NEVER CAUGHT UP*

EGGS IN A BASKET

Once you have your emergency fund of three to six months income in place you should begin to look at diversifying. The financial community talks of not having all your eggs in one basket. (Probably because sometimes the financial community drops the basket). The concept of spreading your investments to avoid risk is very good. After you have your foundation laid you should be careful not to leave all or the majority of your wealth in one institution or even one type of investment. Be careful not to attempt to get too fancy too soon. Unless you have at least $15,000, just keep it in your local bank or money market and be boring. But, if you are saving actively, and applying some of our principles, you very quickly will have more than that to watch over.

You are, as of this writing, insured in FDIC banks to $100,000 per individual, but that is not to say that you should have all of your funds in one institution. If your FDIC bank fails, and many of them have, you will get your money. The problem is it may be months or even years before the FDIC pays on their insurance. Never bank in only one place. Your banker will not like that advice!

Never have all your money in real estate, or the stock market, or money markets, or in any one place. As your cash stash increases, you can get very sophisticated in your approach, but beware that simplicity will usually win out over even the most learned advice when it comes to personal money management.

ATTITUDE IS EVERYTHING

Also be aware of your attitude as your cash increases. I have repeatedly said that "money is active", even in the spiritual sense. Be careful that you continue to own your money and that as it grows it never begins to own you. Larry Burkett, in his series called "*How to Manage Your Money*" says, "attitude is the only difference between saving and hoarding."

We are beginning to have some fun with this money management "*stuff*". You see the power that it can have in your finances as you take control instead of it having control of you. If you will heed the power of compound interest and have it work for you, you will go from fun to fantasy in the next chapter.

Proverbs 21:20 says "IN THE HOUSE OF THE WISE ARE STORES OF CHOICE FOOD AND OIL, But a foolish man devours all he has."

PEACE PUPPIES

1) Avoid "Stuffitis"-The Worship of "Stuff"
2) Plant Seeds-Give Money Away To Worthy Causes
3) Develop Your Own "Power Over Purchase"
4) Find What You Are Naturally Gifted At, Enjoy Your
   Work, And Work Hard
5) Live Substantially Below Your Income
6) Sacrifice Now So You Can Have Peace Later
7) You Can Always Spend More Than You Can Make
8) You Must Save Money (The Power Of Compound
   Interest)

CHAPTER NINE

BUY ONLY BIG BIG BARGAINS

Fun, Fun, Fun, FUN. That is what getting a great buy on something of good quality that you really need is, it is just plain F-U-N. This is the most fun of the basic principles we will cover. After all that discipline, let's go and get a "steal" of a deal!!!

Three essential things you must understand in hunting big game, like "Big Bargains" are: you must learn to negotiate; you must learn where to find bargains; and you must have patience. We will discuss each one in detail.

EVERYTHING, I MEAN EVERYTHING

First, you must learn to negotiate EVERYTHING. Everything you buy is negotiable at some time, at some place, and you must find it. The days of impulse buying are over, and the days of negotiation are in for the people who want to get control of their financial life.

Most people are very anti-confrontational by nature. Most of us, even the boisterous and outgoing, do not want head-to-head confrontation. If you understand that people do not want to meet head-on, it will aid you in your negotiations. If you will approach your purchases hunting a way to win for everyone, you will buy things very cheaply. If someone needs to sell very badly, you have helped him by making that purchase. But you must win too, and your winning can occur in the area of price or terms.

THE WAY TO DO WIN WIN

In "Getting to Yes", a book by Roger Fisher and William Ury of the Harvard Negotiation Project, they tell the classic story illustrating that everyone can win in a negotiation: "There were once two elderly ladies who had one orange between them which they were negotiating for. After lengthy discussion these two ladies could not come up with a solution except to split the difference, so they cut the orange in half each taking one half. One lady proceeded to peel the orange and use the peel for baking a cake, while the other peeled her half and ate the fruit." If the two had spent time finding out, through good communication, what their needs were for the orange they both could have had the whole orange, and neither would have been the lesser. If you will bring creativity and communication to your purchases you can make excellent buys and help people in the process.

I MEAN EVERYTHING

You must negotiate with everyone. Two major pizza chains in our area are competing aggressively for their share of the market. My family prefers the taste of one brand better, but the other brand runs better advertised specials. My wife determined to get the brand we wanted at the other's price, so she called to place the order and told our brand if they wanted the business they would have to match the other brand's price. At first they did not want to, because there was a good bit of price difference, but when my wife explained that she would simply call the other brand, and place an order, they very happily gave us the good pizza at the good price. Our family does this just for the fun of it.

I do not buy a car stereo off the showroom floor, I want them to bring the one from the back with a small scratch and I will save $200. I buy kitchen appliances, cars, clothes, everything at discount simply because I have the nerve to ask.

EVERYONE ELSE DOES

If you have ever visited any foreign country you know that "the market place" and haggling is a way of life for all the rest of the world. But not us. Oh no! We have to go to the shining shopping mall and pay full retail with mark up plus, and charge it at

18% interest or we are not happy. It is time to change !!! We must start today to do things differently.

TRADE

Another method of negotiating is to trade. You can trade goods or services you have for others' goods or services if you will just remember to ask. I have traded two .22 rifles, that I paid $10 apiece for and had never shot in 5 years, for $100 worth of landscaping. I have traded stock for real estate, and land for houses, etc. I have traded a small consulting job of two hours for new carpet (top quality) in my den. Young couples trying to get started can trade painting or yard work for rent or for a down payment on a first home. If you will just think, you will find you have services and goods of value that someone else needs, and you have a potential trade.

THE BASICS

When you begin this process of negotiating, simply stay calm, and use some basic principles. While negotiating can be a very complex and detailed science, in normal consumer purchases you will only meet about 2% of the people who understand and implement what I call the "lucky seven" basic principles of negotiating.

1) ALWAYS TELL THE TRUTH

There is never enough money to be made, or lost, on a deal to warrant a lack of integrity. We as a society seem to have lost this simple and yet far reaching and profound principle.

2) USE THE POWER OF CASH

Now that you have saved some money from the last chapter, let's explore just how much negotiating power that has given you. Not only have you saved money, and used compound interest in your favor, but now you get to see the real benefit. People get silly when they see cash, not a check, or bank note, CASH. There is something highly emotional about flashing cash when making a purchase. If you are buying a car from an individual, and you have thoroughly checked it out, and are ready to make an offer, do it in cash. If you will count out slowly, with drama, $5,000 in $100 bills on his trunk lid, you can often buy that car he is asking $7,000 for. People react to the surety and the instancy of CASH. If you are buying a $2,000 computer, use cash visually when discussing what you will pay for it. You will get a discount. I have a friend that buys foreclosure real estate with cash in small denominations. He gets a $19 brief case with loud latches, fills it with $50,000 in $20 bills, opens it with great fanfare, and says "Here is my offer, $50,000." You would not believe the stories he tells as to reaction, but he gets great buys on real estate.

3) UNDERSTAND AND USE "WALK AWAY POWER"

You must be prepared to walk away and not make the purchase. If the seller senses, and he can, that you are married to that purchase you will receive no discounts. Sometimes this is not a bluff and you must simply walk away to buy another day. Do not get married to someone's product or service before the transaction is complete. I know of irreputable real estate people who wait until you sit down to sign the closing papers on the house, and then change the deal. They figure no one will back out at that point and they are usually right.

4) SHUT UP

You talk too much. We all talk too much. When faced with a purchase, we sense the inherent confrontation, we get nervous, and talk too much. Even the big-time pro negotiators do this. If you will simply shut-up, people will talk themselves OUT of more than you will ever talk them into. Just make small comments and let them rattle. Like "Joe, it seems that your price is possibly too high". Then shut-up and see just how far he will talk *himself* down.

5) *"THAT IS NOT GOOD ENOUGH"*

It is said that Henry Kissinger once asked a member of his staff to research a particular subject and write a paper on it. After six months of research and writing, the staffer set the document on his desk for Kissinger's approval. The staffer received the report back the next day with "You'll have to do better, this is not good enough" written across it. So the staffer spent another three months doing further research and resubmitted his report only to have it returned the next day with the same words across it.

Once again the staffer went to work and spent another month fine tuning his findings. This time out of exasperation he personally took the paper to Kissinger, telling him there was positively nothing further to be learned on this subject on planet earth. Kissinger then responded, "Good, NOW I will read it..", Kissinger knew that everyone has more room to expand or reduce anything, and the same principle holds true when negotiating. When the price is given reply with, "That is not good enough, what can you really do?" You will see the price drop, sometimes lower than you would have offered. Instead of giving a lower offer, try using that verbiage.

6) GOOD GUY - BAD GUY

Your wife or husband, who is not with you, should always seem mean to the other side. "My wife would kill me if I took that price" or "You know, my husband doesn't like it if I come home with a new dress if I didn't get a good buy." You should always use this and be very aware that it is used against you by retailers. They call it "position selling," but I am sure you have heard a salesman say, "Let me check with my manager on your offer." When he comes back the manager who has one eye in the center of his head and foams at the mouth just won't go along with your offer, but he will let you buy today, and today only, at blank price. Do not let them use it on you. Note: when you are using this technique you *must* be telling the truth.

7) "IF I" GIVE, BUT TAKE

When you reach a point that you must give up something, be sure you take something while you are doing that. You should say "IF I" give you $2,500 for that entertainment center, then you have to throw in the cabinet (or something) and the sales tax at no extra charge." You must not just give. Instead, always make your giving contingent upon your receiving something else. "Mommy I want that toy." "Sure son, if you clean up your room." Works everywhere doesn't it?

NOW DO IT

That is the "lucky seven." It is fun to negotiate, and I have used small dollar examples. I have, however, used these same principles on million dollar real estate deals and they still work. You must look for the way everyone can win and then begin to explore and ask questions. Keep your eyes open and you can have a lot of fun with this. You will never get peace in your finances until you learn to buy at bargains and to do that you must employ at least basic negotiating principles.

1) ALWAYS TELL THE TRUTH
2) USE THE POWER OF CASH
3) UNDERSTAND AND USE
   "WALK AWAY POWER"
4) SHUT UP
5) "THAT IS NOT GOOD ENOUGH"
6) GOOD GUY - BAD GUY
7) "IF I" GIVE, BUT TAKE

THE HUNT

The second element you must understand to get great buys is they are sometimes buried treasure. You must hunt far and wide for that really good deal. To purchase an $18,000 car for $11,000, you do not look in the dealer ads in the newspaper. Deals like that do not get advertised by dealers. They buy them, and sell to you at retail.

INDIVIDUALS

Individuals are a good place to make great buys. They have a reason to sell now and are seldom motivated by profit, but more by a need to turn that item into something they need, like cash. The "power of cash" is particularly strong with individuals selling slightly used items they no longer want or need. They are more likely to have fewer defenses to basic negotiating and feel the pressure of your walking away much more than a retail business.

I do not buy cars from dealers. You are welcome to do so, someone has to buy new cars, but I will never again pay retail for an item that depreciates by huge percentages in the first year. I have heard the pitch that the luxury cars of Brand X and Brand Z hold their sticker price better than the others, but one is merely lousy and the other is double lousy. I buy cars at repossession auctions and from individuals. Most states require banks to sell the cars that they repo at some sort of public sale. These sales are conducted many different ways, but many areas sell at public auction. The cars are often dirty, very dirty, maybe have flat tires and dead batteries, but at the right price you can afford to buy a battery.

I purchased a Lincoln Continental worth $18,000 for $11,000 for my wife. The battery was dead and it was filthy, but that scared off other bidders. After a new battery and a detailed clean-up, and we had a "steal" of a car. You must have cash or certified funds to bid it most of these sales, and you need to beware of serious mechanical problems, but there are great car buys to be had.

PUBLIC AUCTIONS

Almost anything you could wish to purchase is sold at estate sales and bankruptcy sales. Many times even brand new items are liquidated at low prices to settle estates of probate and bankruptcy. I needed a microfiche reader for my office, and after finding the price to be $400 from the dealer, I proceeded to buy a slightly used one from the classified ads for $125, after negotiating and using the "power of cash." Shortly after that, a business friend needed a reader also, but was able to buy it for $10 at a bankruptcy auction. I guess he won that one.

I needed to replace the copier for my offices so I began to shop my usual haunts to find a bargain. I went to a bankruptcy auction to watch a large law firm being liquidated which had 10 copiers to be sold. They were all bringing more money than I would bid, until the last one. The best was saved for last. A copier with all the bells and whistles that sold for over $5,000 new came up for sale, and the auctioneer in his haste didn't get the power cord plugged in properly, so the power did not come on. Since the power didn't come on, the auctioneer said, "Well, it will make a good boat anchor." The end of the story is I bought it for $225, had it delivered to my office, and plugged it in where it still works perfectly to this day.

Auctions are great places to get good buys. Be careful not to get caught up in the excitement of the sale and bid too much. It is the auctioneer's job to hype the sale and get as much adrenaline flowing as possible. Also, understand that only "absolute" auctions sell at the price sold. If the auction is not absolute the seller has reserved the right to reject your bid.

GARAGE SALES AND FLEA MARKETS

Garage sales and flea markets are also places to find good buys. You will usually have to look at a lot of junk that you do not need. I have seen hundreds of popcorn poppers for sale, but you can get good buys on high quality items. I go to garage sales in the affluent areas of town and find very nice items. A close friend in the financial planning business recently bought 20 custom made $85 shirts for $1.50 each that had only been worn once. The man selling them had gained weight and could not wear them anymore. $1700 worth of top line dress shirts for $30 is a good garage sale buy. At flea markets and garage sales do not forget to negotiate and use the power of cash. This is a good place to practice your new negotiating skills without much risk, so when the large items come along you have had some practice.

CLASSIFIED ADS

The classified ad section of your newspaper is a good way to find bargains. Plus, most major cities now have papers devoted exclusively to classified ads that only sell items for individuals. Both of these should be considered excellent sources for good buys. Everyone wanting to sell something is not a potential great buy, so look for the right ads like "must sell" or "owner desperate." If you find ads that read this way, call and find out the reason for selling which should tell you just how "desperate" the owner really is. You should try to find individuals here who are motivated sellers, because what you need is a great buy.

In recent years buying on the warehouse concept through large consumer warehouses has become popular. These companies will sell to you in large volume and at purported savings. Be careful. While there are many good buys in these volume purchases, some items are priced even higher than retail stores. And many times you will not use the volume required for three or four years and that is not a good bargain.

COUPONS

Another place I use to get bargains is coupon clipping. This seems so minor when you look at saving 20 cents, but my wife saved over $600 last year using coupons. Do not buy what you do not need. Instead, only use the coupons on items that you would buy anyway and look for merchants that offer "double your coupon" days for extra savings. Just a few minutes a week and buying your food with a plan will save you many dollars.

Bargain hunting at outlet stores and at sales is the least effective, but many times, if you are very careful and don't forget to ask for a lower price, even these retailers will sell cheap. When a particular store is moving or has a seasonal close-out on clothing use the cash-on-the-counter routine and ask that commissioned sales clerk how much price she will cut if you buy several dresses. The point here is that you waited, watched, then acted for the bargain.

REAL ESTATE BARGAINS

Real estate can be a real bargain today if you watch what you are doing. For years I have bought foreclosures and have made many excellent buys. Many times I have bought houses worth $50,000 for less than $20,000. Buying foreclosures, after they have been foreclosed on, from HUD or VA, or the bank that foreclosed, can give you thousands of dollars in savings. Be extremely careful, and use a good attorney who specializes in real estate, if you are going to buy at actual foreclosure sales at the courthouse steps. There are many ways to get in deep trouble here, unlike what some of the tape gurus tell us. This is a very technical business, but if you buy after the foreclosure you can still get great buys without as much risk. Many times you will have to overlook some dirty carpet that needs replacing, walls that need painting, and grass waist high, but for a $20,000 savings you should be able to live with that.

OWNER FINANCING BONANZA

Possibly the most overlooked hidden treasure is in your current home mortgage. When you bought your home did you get owner financing? If you did, you may very well be able to save tens of thousands of dollars. As this century closes, we are seeing fewer and fewer people who have cash. Most people need cash.

If you bought your house for $120,000 with $20,000 down and the original owner carried a mortgage of $100,000 for you, then you should make him a low offer for early pay-off. If he tries to sell that mortgage to raise cash he would have trouble getting $70,000 cash for it. I recommend that you call him and make him an offer to pay him off early at $65,000 cash in the next 30 days subject to your ability to gather up the cash. (Note: This technique will not likely work if you just made the purchase.)

If he only agrees to accept $80,000 after negotiation, then get this agreement in writing. Next, arrange to refinance at $80,000 with a mortgage company. When your loan is approved, and you pay him off, you have just made $20,000. However, do not use this technique to get a $100,000 loan and pocket $20,000. Even if the mortgage company will let you, it is still not the purpose of this suggestion. The purpose is to see you free, not bound to high payments. You have effectively bought this $120,000 house for $100,000. In a cash poor society you will be amazed how many individual mortgage holders will deeply discount their mortgage notes for quick cash.

There are bargains everywhere if we just take time to look. Do not get the idea that only junk can be bought at a bargain. Remember, I like only good *"stuff"*. Train yourself to search out and then negotiate for these great buys.

WAITING IS SO HARD

Once you have learned basic negotiation technique and learned where to find great buys, you need to take the final and toughest step to being a big game "Bargain Hunter". You must learn patience. Well, here is another financial rule that requires discipline. Many times if you have the negotiation skills and have looked in the right places, but have no patience, you will still miss the bargain.

If you have sweated and strained to save save save, as we outlined in the last chapter, you have the cash. If you then get buyer's fever, and run right out and make the first or second purchase you see, you very likely will have missed the best buy.

THIS WAS REALLY FUN

Years ago, when Houston, Texas and other oil cities were having serious economic trouble, the high priced luxury car market was deeply depressed. I decided during that time that I had to have a Jaguar automobile. I ended up buying a Jag in excellent condition with low miles, on a Monday night in the rain, for $21,000. At that time it had a retail value of $29,000. I saved $8,000! I bought it from a real estate developer who would loose it to the bank on Friday if I did not buy it that week. He was motivated, and very happy to see me, and my cash. The reason I am telling you about this purchase, is it took me six months to find the right price on the right car. I subscribed to the Houston newspaper and cut out the Jag ads everyday, and called them for six months, before getting the great buy I needed. You have to have patience.

WHAT A BOSS

I had an administrative assistant working with our team years ago who was renting her home and wanted to buy a home. Because she waited almost one year we were able to get that young couple in their 20's a house that appraised for $134,000 for $58,300. That is a great buy !!!!, but it took patience. Believe me, that young couple had a hard time waiting that whole year, not knowing when they would find the right deal, but it appears to have been worth it.

While writing this chapter my personal car has been totaled and now I am hunting for another car. I now know *again* that it is hard to wait and look for just that right buy. I am experiencing first hand, again, that getting that great buy is a hassle, but my experience reminds me every morning that patience, persistence, and cash will help me "steal" a deal.

Recently I taught these concepts in a seminar. One week later a young person in his 20's called me to tell me about two possible car purchases that he had found and wanted to know which I thought he should buy. After a lengthy conversation I realized that he had the car fever real bad, which meant that patience and walk-away negotiating power were gone. I did not advise which car to buy, because those are not the only two cars in the world for sale, and neither looked like a particularly good buy.

CHILL OUT

Do not get the fever!!! When you get the fever you loose all patience and negotiating power. Pretend that all these purchases are a game, and have some fun with it, because the retail people selling you are definitely having fun.

We must begin to think like vultures. Nice vultures, but still vultures. Now vultures are not very pretty, but the patience displayed by this animal in the wild is something we should observe. The cartoon of the two vultures on a limb with one saying "Patience my tail, I'm gonna kill something" describes most of our buying habits, but we must change to real patience.

You can have some great fun in this area of getting great buys. The more great buys you get, the more fun you will have, and the more confidence you will have in these principles. I will not tell you that these great buys are on every corner, but if you will work at negotiating, hunting buried treasure, and having patience, you will change your cash outflow dramatically. When your cash outflow is decreased, you can save even more. Then you can get even better buys. And then save more, and so on goes the spiral of financial peace. Go for it!

PEACE PUPPIES

1) Avoid "Stuffitis"-The Worship of "Stuff"

2) Plant Seeds-Give Money Away To Worthy Causes

3) Develop Your Own "Power Over Purchase"

4) Find What You Are Naturally Gifted At, Enjoy Your Work, And Work Hard

5) Live Substantially Below Your Income

6) Sacrifice Now So You Can Have Peace Later

7) You Can Always Spend More Than You Can Make

8) You Must Save Money (The Power Of Compound Interest)

9) Learn Basic Negotiating Skills For Great Buys

10) Learn Where To Find Great Buys(The Treasure Hunt)

11) You Must Have Patience To Get Great Buys

CHAPTER TEN

DON'T DO DEBT

The toughest job of persuasion I have in this entire book comes in this chapter. Imagine that once upon a time you were driving down a dark interstate late at night. It begins to snow, making the roads very slick, and just as you remember the weatherman warned of record sub-zero temperatures your car begins to lose hold on the road. You are a young and inexperienced driver, you lose control and go down a ravine, striking a tree at the bottom of the ravine. When you hit the tree your car wraps around you injuring you severely. Because of the snowstorm it takes too long for rescuers to find you, and you get frostbite in your hands and feet.

THIS IS A YUCKY STORY

You wake up days later in a hospital alive, but horrified to find that you have lost one hand and one foot due to the wreck and the frostbite. The doctor says you will have a recovery time of at least six weeks in the hospital.

Don't Do Debt

While you are recovering, you begin to study auto accidents from all vantage points. You keep the library busy bringing you research material and you discover startling new statistics regarding the number of injuries in autos. You read everything you can find on cars, good and bad. While lying there with the physical and emotional pain caused by a car, you pick up this book, and through very persuasive arguments I convince you that driving a car is a mistake. You decide to give up the practice of owning, driving, or even riding in, an automobile.

You announce your intentions to your family and friends and get reactions of scorn and shock. They try to convince you that only a fool would refuse to use such a wonderful convenience. Some even think the wreck has affected you mentally.   THE END

I HOPE THERE IS A POINT TO THAT STORY

I am not going to say that you should not drive cars, but I am going to ask you to consider something that will seem just as ridiculous and un-American. Some of you have been in a "financial wreck" that ripped pain through your family, and your soul, causing permanent scars. Some have even lost a spouse due to the financial stress. You will be reading with an open mind, but some of you have never even had a small dent in your financial car door. So you will probably not even read this whole chapter, and you will likely view me as having little sense. What I have to report to you, from observing national trends and people in pain, is going to be just as hard to swallow as my telling you not to drive cars. Never-the-less, I am duty bound to tell you:

DON'T DO DEBT. That's right, do not borrow money.

YOU COMMUNIST!!

You may say, "What?! How un-American! Only Communists don't borrow money! How can a capital-driven society possibly survive if there is no debt?" Well, it can survive and you can survive, *ye* even prosper! This problem of consumers, companies, and even nations loading themselves with debt is an aggressive, fast spreading, and financially deadly cancer. I refer you to your own budget and to the statistics earlier in the book. We borrow as if we have forgotten that we have to pay it back. WE DO! Look at it from the positive side; if you had no debt, how much money could you save every month? If you look at what we have learned about compound interest and bargain hunting, with a totally freed up budget you could be wealthy, wildly wealthy, within just a few years, but we are strapped with debt.

Proverbs 22:7 The rich rule over the poor and **THE BORROWER IS SERVANT TO THE LENDER.**

We as consumers have become a nation of servants to financial institutions. We used to joke that a bank was where you could borrow money if you could prove you didn't need it. Now, with the advent of aggressive credit marketing strategies we can borrow even when we shouldn't be allowed too. We are sold credit in so many ways by so many people that we end up buying *a lot* of it, meaning we borrow money. We borrow money, not just because it is made easy for us, but because we are sold on the convenience, perceived prosperity, and fun that all that *"stuff"* and associated debt, are supposed to bring us. Let's look at some of these financial products and discover where we *really* are with them.

THE REST OF THE STORY

I mean we are getting in deep. *Consumer Reports Complete Guide to Managing Your Money* states that the typical household debt totals more than $23,000. The total consumer debt in the United States is over $2 trillion with a "t". Of which about $1.5 trillion is in mortgage debt, $192 billion in auto loans, $175 billion in personal loans. In addition Bankcard Holders of America says that we have over $200

billion charged to our 600 million credit cards at an
average rate of 19.5%. Even in spite of this some of
you are sitting there shaking your head at this poor
backwoods thinking author for suggesting something
as radical as no debt. But of course *you* would never
abuse borrowing, seems that I heard an alcoholic tell
me that once about drinking.

CREDIT CARDS

The easiest to convince you not to use is credit
cards. The typical card holder carries 5 to 7 cards
that were accumulated by no more logic than just
who sent him one. Many an expert has written on the
evils of credit cards. They are dangerous and
horrible financial tools. The convenience of plastic
makes you buy *"stuff"* you would never buy
otherwise. The advertisements purport that you will
have more social status, glamor, and fun by using
their super platinum gold titanium card. I remember
years ago when I got my first American Express
Gold Card, I really thought I was hot stuff. If your
self esteem is drawn from the metal of your plastic
you have missed the boat. Go home.

HAVING FUN YET?

You get the *perceived plastic prosperity* disease
where you appear prosperous, but are digging a
grave. You see no cash pass from your hand, and so

you register very little emotional realization that you just spent money.

The interest rates are at the rape level. In 1991 the credit card industry had revenues of over $34 billion according to Bankcard Holders of America. When you add the annual fees, and other garbage charged to you, the effective rate on your borrowed money is ridiculous. I think after looking at it from the bank's side I will start a DaveCard. Want one?

How many times have you gone out to eat, or bought clothes, or even taken a vacation that you could not afford, but borrowed the money through plastic purchases at lousy rates and terms? I have done it, and so have most of you, but this is bad, bad planning and use of your funds. I have not had a credit card for years now. Many people tell me that they can control it. Therapists who specialize in addictions say that the first level of treatment always involves denial which they consider to be a strong indicator that there is an addictive problem.

MORE SAD STUFF

I recently counseled a couple in their 40's who had been married for over 15 years. These were very upright moral people who had a little trouble with their finances. He had been laid off, but they maintained their two-income lifestyle accumulating $50,000 in credit card debt. When they could not pay the monthly bills they came to us for help. In over 15 years they had never been one day late on a payment to anyone, but now they were committed to $3,200 more per month than they had coming in.

They ended up losing everything they owned. They are now starting over. They still love each other, fortunately, and they will make it, but it is a shame they have that emotional scar to live with the rest of their lives. Please don't tell me you can control your plastic, because I have seen too much pain that proves otherwise. Stop reading now and cut them up.

HOME EQUITY LOANS

The latest rage on the credit scene is home equity loans. Current tax law makes it advantageous tax-wise to borrow on your home rather than on other goods. Have you forgotten that this is your home, you know, basic needs, like shelter? Many Americans currently have a roof over their family, but will risk that just for the sake of sophistication, tax advantage, or worse yet a vacation like the ads call for. Amazing what a tax law change followed by a little marketing will do to our sensibilities. As real estate has declined in value in many areas we need to remember that we might have to end up writing a check in order to sell that home someday. Many noted publications have said home equity loans are the next big downfall of the consumer, and I am beginning to see too many in foreclosure. Beware!

REGULAR MORTGAGES

Regular home loans are probably the best buy you can get, in general. The interest rates and terms are about the best of any borrowing available to the consumer. The worst home loans are the Adjustable Rate Mortgages or ARMs. These mortgages normally adjust annually based on what another rate does. Most of these adjustments are based on indexes like the one-year treasury bills (T Bills) or on the 11th district cost of funds index for the Federal Home Loan Bank Board.

The T-bill is the more volatile of the two, but neither is acceptable in terms of risk. The Wall Street Journal has reported that many financial institutions "forget" to lower the rate.(strange how they never "forget" to raise it). A fixed-rate shorter term loan on a home is your best bet, and I will expand on that later.

AUTO LOANS

Auto loans are terrible because, unless on a very short term (3 years or less), the value of the car normally drops much faster than the loan balance, leaving you in a precarious position. Most auto loans go far too long and charge a premium interest rate as opposed to prime. Plus when you finance a car you cannot get as good a buy, so you are paying extra again.

The worst deal on the car lot today is the car lease. Most auto leases by the major companies are currently figured on an 18% yield based on what the car will be worth at the end of the lease. You are paying within a few dollars per month of a straight finance plan and do not own the car at the end of the term. Possibly the worst feature of most leases is you are trapped for the period of the lease and most families trade cars more often than 5 or 7 years. Yes, you can trade with that dealer and many times get out of the lease for a penalty, but again you are paying a premium.

You do not have to borrow money to buy a car. Pay cash for one that is not quite what you want and start saving the equivalent of a car payment a month, and very soon you can drive whatever you want. By sniffing out great deals and selling every so often I drive almost free. I'll bet you agree that "free" beats a lease.

ANATOMY OF A REPO

Let's look at what can happen to you if you have financial problems after financing a new car. If you buy a new $18,000 car and finance it for 7 years at 13%, payments will be $327 per month. What happens if you get laid off after one year of ownership and cannot pay the payments? The car is now worth an average of $13,000, but you owe $16,800. You cannot sell it for what you owe, and they repossess it.

When they sell it on the repo lot it will bring about $9,000, leaving you still owing $7,800 which they will chase you to the ends of the earth for. You may be able to settle with them on this $7,800 deficit by making payments, if you are lucky. But, it is very hard to make payments on a car you no longer own. I have met many people who have had to endure this scenario.

Foreclosure on a house creates a similar situation, except you can add a zero to the end of the figure causing the problem. There are many bankruptcies filed every year due to this leftover debt after repo.

Many say "How could the bank possibly expect me to pay the difference?" Simple, because you signed a loan agreement obligating yourself personally. This is called personal liability, which means regardless of what happens to the item you pledged for the loan (the collateral) you still owe the money. If they don't get enough from the collateral you are legally obligated for the balance.

Should you total the car in a wreck, and owe more than what the car is worth, in all likelihood you will get an insurance check for the value and you will still owe the difference. I have seen this problem more than once. Most people have no idea what those loan agreements mean that they are signing. Because you are personally liable, if you do not pay that balance (called a deficit), the lender will sue you for it, and they will win the suit.

THEN IT REALLY GETS ROUGH

Upon winning the suit, if you still cannot pay, they will execute on the suit. Which means that they will begin to collect things of yours to sell, and the proceeds are applied to the balance. They will attach, and clean out, savings and checking accounts. They will garnishee your wages, meaning the court orders your employer to pay the court the majority of your check until you have paid the balance. They can come to your home with a warrant and take your furniture, including your baby bed, and sell it to pay on your balance. You will truly begin to see that the *borrower is the servant to the lender.*

Should you happen to have an account with the bank that you defaulted on, the loan agreement you signed probably gives them the right to clean out that account without even a lawsuit and apply that money to your deficit balance. If you have other loans with the bank in default and pay your car off they probably do not have to give you the title until all loans are paid in full, due to what is called a "dragnet clause" in the loan document.

Basically if you do not pay on any loan they will own you until you do. The only escape is payment or bankruptcy. The laws and mechanics for collection of defaulted loans may differ slightly in your state from listed above, but they will collect somehow, unless you file bankruptcy. Benjamin Franklin said, "Creditors have better memories than debtors."

FINANCE COMPANIES AND THRIFTS

Perhaps the most expensive money comes from consumer finance companies. These companies specialize in higher risk loans and charge very high interest rates. If your state does not have a cap on interest rates you will usually find these companies charging up to 25% per year. These are the companies that finance furniture, stereos, waterbeds, appliances, electronic equipment, and so on. If you remember the buyer beware chapter, these companies are the ones that buy the "90-days same as cash" contracts, because you will seldom pay those off in 90 days. Over 70% of them convert to 24% loans with prepayment penalties.

DEBT CONSOLIDATION

These companies also do a lot of debt consolidation or bill consolidation loans. Let's look at a bill consolidation loan for the average couple. Joe and Sue have the following debt they wish to consolidate:

Item	Balance	Payment	Interest Rate
Visa	1200	200	18
MasterCard	1700	250	18
Doctor	400	100	18
Gas Card	600	80	18
Car	6500	270	12
Furniture	3500	175	15
TOTAL	13,900	1075	

WHAT ELSE CAN I DO?

These bills are causing "great stain" for Joe and Sue. If only they could get some relief! So they go to the friendly finance company that will not only lend them enough for the bills, but even a little extra so they will have some extra cash. But let's say they just borrow $13,900 and they want to cut their payments in half so they'll have a payment of $550 per month. They will pay that for 36 months for a total of $19,800. This is an extremely poor program because if they could have just worked extra or figured out any way to hold on for 9 months, everything would be paid except the car and the furniture. The total payments would then be only $445 per month and these two will be paid off in two years instead of three years, and at a lower interest rate. Beware of bill consolidation. There are few cases that justify using this strategy.

THE FRIENDLY LOAN

Have you ever loaned money to or borrowed money from a friend or relative? This is the best way I know to lose a friendship or strain a relationship. The borrower feels awkward even being in the same room with the lender, and if something goes wrong, most friendships are destroyed. That is because we have become the servant or the master, not just "Joe" anymore.

CO-SIGNING, NOT VERY BRIGHT

If you are going to avoid borrowing money, you should definitely avoid co-signing for someone else's loan. When you co-sign, you borrow the money. The professional money lender who is trained when to, and when not to, loan money has decided this person should not borrow right now. However, we in our infinite wisdom know better so we sign for him. Besides we were trying to be helpful. When the loan goes bad the bank comes straight to us, because they know he doesn't have the money. I have co-signed for loans and been co-signed for and almost without fail it got me into trouble both ways. I have learned the hard way, I am here to warn you about the pitfalls of co-signing notes.

FOR THE SOPHISTICATE

Now we have reviewed the major areas and ways to borrow money, let's address one more issue for the finance major who has more sophisticated viewpoints or arguments. Without going into a lengthy and detailed explanation, I have run computer models on debt-free investment analysis. The concept of leverage is always brought up when I talk about being debt free. I have a thorough understanding of Internal Rates of Return, Net Present Value, Simple Return on Investment, and a myriad of other measurements that we are taught show the power of using borrowed money on investments. The interesting thing is that seldom is a risk factor brought into the formula, thereby effectively reducing the perceived yield.

There are sophisticates who want to cross swords on this issue, but I think they will find that a reasonable risk factor (that risk is not present when debt free) reduces the advantages of leverage to zero in a closer look. Also if you have done much business with European or Mid-eastern companies you will find they exist on virtually no debt and do just fine. In our arrogance we think the "big crash" will never happen to us. Wrong.

I counseled a very sophisticated investor recently who had a large net worth at one time. He had borrowed $70,000 from a local bank to purchase two limited partnership shares in a real estate deal. The real estate company he purchased them through was nationally known and the largest in the Southeast. That company had been open for many years with a wonderful track record. They almost never lost money. In fact, they almost always exceeded the projected returns.

The horribly negative impact that the 1986 Tax Act had on the real estate world broke that company. That left the partners trying to run a large apartment complex in a metropolitan city 500 miles away. They had leveraged into the deal (borrowed all they could) so there was very little equity, and with the downfall of income-producing real estate prices, the apartment complex actually became worth less than the mortgages. With negative equity the two limited partnership shares he had purchased to save on taxes and make money with were now worthless, but he still owed money on them. So he now owes the bank a $70,000 unsecured loan. He is having trouble paying that loan and will likely go into default. But, he could "control" it or so he thought.

YOU REALLY COME OUT MUCH BETTER

Author Robert Ringer tells the story of a recently deceased friend of his who had the same horrible experience in the Great Depression of the 1930s that many people are having today. His personal home was foreclosed on and he had to start completely over. Because of the pain this man vowed to NEVER borrow money again from anyone. Over his lifetime he built a substantial fortune, and as his cash position grew his fortune grew faster and faster. His wealth grew at explosive rates because he never had losses due to payments, and because during down times he always had cash to make the great buys from distressed sellers. He bought office buildings, office equipment, cars, homes, and even entire companies for CASH, always getting substantial discounts. At his death he was worth in excess of 500 million dollars. Don't tell me it doesn't work!

IF YOU MUST

After all that, if you must borrow money, let me give you two basic guidelines. First, borrow on short terms and only borrow on items that go up in value. That means you never borrow on any consumer items except a home. Then the terms are very important. If you can, buy less, so that you can pay off faster, and then make sure you get a very low interest rate. Example: if you were to finance $80,000 on a home at 10%, here are two ways:

30 years 300 payments at $702/mo $252,720 total
15 years 180 payments at $860/mo $154,800 total
Total difference $158 more, but $97,920 saved

Be careful because well meaning, well trained real estate brokers will sell you all you can possibly afford on a 30 year mortgage. They get paid on a percentage of the sales price, not on how much you save over 15 years. Be sure you remember how much you save if you go with shorter terms.

If you already have your 30 year mortgage in place, just pay one or two extra payments per year to be applied to principal. For example, a $100,000, 30 year mortgage at 10%, will pay off in 18.8 years just by paying one extra payment per year.

OK, I GIVE, NOW WHAT

You say "Okay, okay, you win I want out of debt and I want to stay out, but how do I do that?" There are two things you can do. The first method took years of research and many hours of development to get the concept in place. This highly sophisticated concept is top secret and is usually reserved for very special situations only. This first method to get out of debt is:

"In order to get out of debt:
quit borrowing more money. "

Our problem is not getting out of debt it is keeping out of debt. Almost all consumer loans are set up to pay off naturally, and just by paying the payments you will soon be completely debt free.

THE DEBT SNOWBALL

The second way out involves accelerating the process. I first learned this technique through Larry Burkett's Christian Financial Concepts, but it is taught by many counselors concerned with debt reduction. We call this the "debt snowball." For example let's look at another possible list of debts for Joe and Sue.

Item	Balance	Payment	Rate
Visa	1,200	200	18%
Student Loan	7,000	123	9%
Car	6,500	250	12%
MasterCard	700	70	18%
Gas Card	400	60	18%
House	60,000	540	9%

The first step in this strategy is to put the debts in ascending order with the smallest remaining balance first and the largest last. Do this regardless of interest rate or payment. We will pay these off in this new order. I have read and found in actual experience that this works because you get to see some success quickly and are not trying to pay off the largest balance just because it has a high rate of interest. So our new order of attack will look like this:

Item	Balance	Payment	Rate
Gas Card	400	60	18%
MasterCard	700	70	18%
Visa	1,200	200	18%
Car	6,500	250	12%
Student Loan	7,000	123	9%
House	60,000	540	9%

Pretend you're Joe, and I'll show you how this strategy works. Now Joe decides to work some overtime or Sue has a garage sale and you pay off the gas card in the first month. Next, **DO NOT** spend the $60 per month you used to spend on the gas card, instead add $60 to the next payment on the list. You are then paying MasterCard $130 per month until paid. That will pay off in the 7th month then you add $130 to the $200 Visa payment so that you are paying $330. Because you have already been paying on Visa for 7 months, it will pay off in the 8th month (the next month). So you add $330 to your car payment of $250 making your car payment $580. That will cause the car to be paid off in 17 more months, only 25 months into our program. The happy ending of your story is that everything in our example (and yours will vary) is paid off in 32 months except the house.

BIG FUN

Now you have $1,243 per month to pay on the house, and it will be paid for in five more years. As an alternative you could save $275 per month of the $1,243 to purchase a car with cash. When you pay the remaining $968 the house will pay off in just seven years, while the $275 per month saved will grow to $11,490 in just three years at 10% for your cash car purchase.

As these bills are paid off you will feel a peace and a change in your attitude about financial matters. You will begin to realize that they do not "matter" so much. I can speak from experience as I have worked through a very large "debt snowball."

NOW YOU MUST DECIDE

Well, by this point you are either seriously considering what I have outlined in this chapter or you think I am crazy. I challenge you, you have tried it "their" way and it doesn't work. Try this new approach, you may find some very new consequences in your life. I know that suggesting you stay out of debt is radical and may seem utterly ridiculous, but I am tired of seeing grown adults on the brink of suicide, widows left with a legacy of debt, children who are taught by example that if I want it I get it NOW. Don't do debt and if you do, remember you are instantly the servant to the lender.

Proverbs 22:7 The rich rule over the poor and THE BORROWER IS SERVANT TO THE LENDER.

PEACE PUPPIES

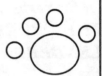

1) Avoid "Stuffitis"-The Worship of "Stuff"

2) Plant Seeds-Give Money Away To Worthy Causes

3) Develop Your Own "Power Over Purchase"

4) Find What You Are Naturally Gifted At, Enjoy Your Work, And Work Hard

5) Live Substantially Below Your Income

6) Sacrifice Now So You Can Have Peace Later

7) You Can Always Spend More Than You Can Make

8) You Must Save Money (The Power Of Compound Interest)

9) Learn Basic Negotiating Skills For Great Buys

10) Learn Where To Find Great Buys(The Treasure Hunt)

11) You Must Have Patience To Get Great Buys

12) The Borrower Is The Servant To The Lender, Beware!!

CHAPTER ELEVEN

"KISS" YOUR MONEY

Years ago, when working daily in personal sales and later in training sales people, we were taught a saying. Most sales people, especially when they are new, talk too much. They talk too much because of their desire to tell the client all the great things about their product or service. Many times a salesperson will talk their client out of the sale by overloading him with information he did not require to make a buying decision.

KEEP IT SIMPLE STUPID

Salespeople have to learn the art of being quiet at the appropriate time and to keep their pitch simple. Because, with the exception of sales on technical products, people know whether they want a product or not after a reasonable amount of information has been presented to them. We were taught the KISS principle to avoid overcomplicating a presentation. KISS stands for KEEP IT SIMPLE, STUPID. We used this bit of comic relief to remind ourselves that it was counterproductive to overcomplicate things. More plainly, it is stupid to over complicate things that do not require it. The handling of money is no exception.

I am not calling anyone stupid so please don't be offended, but you should remember this basic premise. People will lose thousands of dollars to prove they can invest with the sophisticates. I have had people come into my office completely broke with negative monthly budgets and negative net worths and then argue with me about the interest rate on a particular investment. I am continually amazed at all the broke financial geniuses. Our society has made it a sin to make unsophisticated, uncomplicated investments, but it is all right to have zero savings.

WELL I KNOW WHAT I AM DOING

We brag about the investment we made or the great insurance program we have, and if Harry or Jill at work has a better one it is as if we didn't keep up with the Jones. Most of us have gotten so focused on the tax advantages, the get-rich-quick, or the sophistication of the investment, that we forgot to check it against common sense. There is something ridiculously glamorous about investing in something far away with a slick brochure that we don't quite understand. Exotic bird partnerships with tax sheltered 200% returns. Don't you laugh, there are more absurd things out there that sell! Some say,

"Well I know what I am doing." How many times I have heard that. They are the ones about to fall the hardest.

Proverbs 17:12   Let a man meet a bear robbed of her cubs, rather than a fool in his folly.

I REALLY DO KNOW WHAT I AM DOING

I have a close friend who is a fairly wealthy doctor. I have his financial statements and know his business well. I talked with his business administrator at length, and was told the physician's 2.5 million dollar net worth would easily be over 5 million dollars, and largely cash, were it not for one thing. He, like most of us, cannot resist a tax shelter or a great deal on a highly complicated high-return investment. Real estate tax shelters, limited partnerships, bad stock tips, a horrible life insurance product, bad partnerships in other businesses, etc. and etc. have cost him millions of dollars in losses over the past ten years.

His administrator told me that if instead of wacky investments he had saved his cash at only 5%, and just paid his taxes quietly, that he would easily have double what he has now if not three times as much. In his search for financial sophistication he has shot himself in the foot.

YES, BUT THAT IS HIM OR IS IT?

We all do that only in smaller ways. So I will spend the balance of this chapter giving a brief and basic overview of different investments and insurance and hopefully clarify my KISS principle of money. Remember, though, that NO investing in anything short of a savings account should be done until you have three to six months of income for an emergency fund. I have heard it said the safest way to double your money is to fold it over once and put it in your pocket.

THE INFAMOUS STOCK MARKET

First, let's look at the "stock market." Individual stock purchases give you a tiny piece of ownership in a company. You have virtually no say in how the company is run. When you buy stocks you hope to get a return through the stock's increasing in value (purportedly because the company has done well) or through the company's giving its owners (stockholders) some of the profits through paid dividends.

For the part-time investor with his favorite stock broker urging him on, studies have shown the average small portfolio has a return of 7% on a good year. The risk is astronomical for the income earner under $200,000 per year, and given this huge risk and poor offsetting return, individual stock purchases very seldom make sense for the typical family.

Then I have heard, "But what about my grandpa who bought IBM stock for almost nothing in 1965 and got unbelievable returns?" For every IBM story there are hundreds of publicly traded companies in bankruptcy. Stories like IBM are legitimate, but are the exception rather than the rule, and the person who does not research stocks for a living cannot hope to follow the necessary trends and measurements to accurately pick stocks. Even the normal stock broker is taught more about selling than analyzing. Mark Twain summed it up well when he said, "October. This is one of the peculiarly dangerous months to speculate in stocks. The others are July, January, September, April, November, May, March, June, December, August, and February."

BONDS

Individual bond purchases have the same inherent problems and risk. The main difference here is you are a creditor rather than an owner. When you purchase a bond, the company that issued it becomes your debtor. The income is usually fixed, but again the value or price of the bond will go up or down according to the performance of the company and prevailing interest rates. People who have portfolios and attempt to trade individual bonds on a part-time basis or through a stock broker normally have very poor results.

IF YOU MUST

If you view yourself as a part-time wizard of the stock or bond market, I have a challenge for you. USE NO MONEY for this challenge. Use a hypothetical bank account with $200,000 in it and run this challenge for one year starting today. Take your Wall Street Journal and tack it to your dart board. Throw 10 darts at it. Invest 10,000 each (using $100,000) in the ten stocks closest to the darts. With the remaining $100,000 do your best job buying, selling, leveraging, whatever you choose in the New York Stock Exchange for one year. At the end of a year, sell both hypothetical portfolios and see who did the best, you or the dart board. The dart board will beat most of us, and if not, compare your rate of return to conservative investments and you will probably find only a small difference. We will get beat not because we are dumb, but simply because individual stocks selected without thorough investigation (anything short of full time work) tend to do poorly on average.

MUTUAL FUNDS

Mutual funds are the best method of investing in the stock and bond markets for most people. Mutual funds are pools of many individual's (and others) money grouped together for the purchase of certain types of stocks or bonds. As the money is pooled it is invested in many different stocks according to the stated goals of the fund by a fund manager. When you own a mutual fund share, it represents tiny pieces of ownership in hundreds of companies.

You get diversification in mutual funds that you can never achieve in a small or medium sized personal portfolio. You can choose mutual funds that invest in a variety of stocks or specific industry stocks. For example, if you think the healthcare industry is going to expand and be more profitable than most others, then invest in a healthcare industry fund. There are also funds that invest in other types of instruments like bonds or commodities, but at first just keep it simple in a general stock fund. I recommend a general fund with a long track record that has had the same fund manager for a long time. Most stock brokers will not recommend mutual funds because the commissions are usually small. Learn something about these yourself or stay away!! Select by looking at funds with at least a 10 year history of good average annual returns. The top twenty funds have averaged between 20 and 30 percent average annual return. Mutual funds are NOT short-term investments and should be avoided unless you can put your money in and leave it. (interfund transfers for the sophisticate are possible, but this is not to be viewed as a savings account).

ANNUITIES

Annuities are simply savings accounts with a life insurance company or financial institution. They are not insured by the Federal Government, but they usually pay more than banks do on savings accounts. Life insurance companies are not as financially strong as they used to be, so be careful which one you choose. If they go broke, and a few have, you loose your money, all of it.

MUNI-BONDS

Tax Free Municipal Bonds are a good investment for retirees, but again I recommend the use of a mutual fund that invests in these. Cities and states are allowed to issue bonds (borrow money from the purchaser), and the interest that these bonds pay you is tax free. Whatever income you get in the form of interest payments from these tax-free bonds has no federal income tax on it. If the bond pays 5%, and you are in a 30% income tax bracket, you would have to get 7.14% on a Certificate of Deposit to match it after taxes.

ROLLING DICE, COMMODITIES

The purchase of futures or commodities is foolish for the average person. Your chances of hitting the home run you are looking for are better at the roulette table in Las Vegas and I do not recommend either as sound investment strategy.

REAL ESTATE

Real estate investment beyond your personal home has good and bad points. Never invest in real estate without having a substantial cash pad in savings to smooth out the rough months. Responsibility for a bad rental property with no back-up savings has bankrupt many of my clients. Real estate can be a great inflation hedge and can be a good vehicle for amassing wealth from several angles, including cash flow and tax benefits.

The mistake most novice real estate investors make is that they pay too much for properties. DEEP DEEP discounts should be your rule for rental property, and then borrow little or nothing on it. I have seen many people who bought real estate with little or no down payment and paid full appraisal for it. Then the payments are usually more than the rent or slightly less. When the payment is $750 and the rent is $800, you are losing money because of vacancy, maintenance, credit loss (bad tenants), and miscellaneous other draws that the novice overlooks in his purchase.

THAT ELEPHANT HAS TO EAT

Suddenly your glorious method to wealth becomes a white elephant. You owe so much that you cannot afford to sell it and it drains your other assets you've worked so hard to build. Real estate is a legitimate investment, but it should come only after you have accumulated lots of cash. Beware of brokers who know more about selling than they do investments.

SIMPLE DISCIPLINE IS THE KEY

If I sound negative about the investments I've mentioned, it is because I am. I have seen this glass bubble lure people to their financial deaths more times than I've seen their dreams of wealth come true. Remember the quickest way to get rich quick is to NOT get rich quick. Disciplined saving will outpace any investment scheme.

INSURANCE

Another area of complicated financial products is the area of insurance. Let me start out by saying that I'm a firm believer in low cost insurance which provides full coverages. The Bankruptcy Institute says that over 50% of consumer bankruptcies are the result of medical bills of people who have no health insurance. If you do not have health insurance and can get it, do it now. It is financial suicide not to have health and disability insurance. If you have a family, I will go so far as to say it is irresponsible to not have health and disability insurance, if you are not prohibited from obtaining it. It is very expensive, as a matter of fact it is often robbery. But, you can lose a lifetime of work by not having it. Carefully investigate and understand the options so that you know what your coverages are, and then shop around.

Also you should do the same on homeowner's and auto insurance. These policies are more standardized. Most people have them and never use them. Hint: if you have savings, raise your auto and homeowner's deductible to $500 or $1,000, and you will be amazed at the savings on your premium.

LIFE INSURANCE

Life insurance is an area where consumer confusion abounds. Few people understand the policies they own. However, it is irresponsible and poor planning to have no life insurance. The myriad of different insurance programs available boggles the normal consumer's mind. Simply speaking, there are three general types of life insurance in the marketplace today, whole life, universal life, and term. While there are multitudes of variations on these themes, an understanding of these three fundamental types of life insurance will give you insight into the strengths and weaknesses of the programs now available.

WHOLE LIFE

Whole life is death coverage and a built-in savings program. Your premiums are high for the death protection and an unstated amount of the premium is going to build savings called cash value. The return on the savings program is extremely poor, usually around 3%. The industry calls the savings program "cash value" and tempts you into believing that it just appears there because you are a nice person. Wrong! You have paid more than needed to buy the death protection and they have allocated some of the difference to a savings program which pays a poor rate of return.

Let's pick on Joe some more. Joe buys a whole life policy with a face amount of $70,000, then pays on it for ten years and builds up a "cash value" of $8,000. Then something happens to poor Joe. What does the company pay to Sue and the kids? Answer: $70,000. If Joe has been paying too much for insurance for ten years so that he can build cash value, what happened to the cash value (saving at 3%) at Joe's death? His insurance company keeps it. Sounds fair to me! HA! I am strongly against whole life life insurance because I don't like the system under which you are saving and it is expensive.

UNIVERSAL OR VARIABLE LIFE

Universal life is the updated version of whole life. When the insurance companies began to realize that you consumers were catching on to whole life, they tried to make it more palatable. Universal life usually pays a much better interest rate on the savings program, and most now allow your beneficiary (spouse) to get the face amount PLUS the savings account (cash value) at death. So what is wrong with this? The cost of the pure insurance inside the plan is normally high, and therefore less of your premium is going to savings. The savings, while it does better than whole life, seldom reaches the "projected rate" you were sold of 10% to 15%. If we judge the savings portion like we judge a mutual fund, on its track record, it will not even stack up to a Certificate of Deposit. So what we end up with is expensive insurance and a mediocre savings program. Why would a company out for profit ever offer to help you save money if they did not make a profit from doing so? Beware of any life insurance that has a built-in saving program.

TERM, LEVEL TERM

Term life insurance is pure insurance. You are getting no savings program, which is good news after looking at the last two. Term is like your auto or homeowner's insurance. If the event occurs the insurance company pays. Simple, no bells, no whistles. I, like most competent financial planners, recommend the purchase of low cost level term insurance for 10 to 20 years (guaranteed renewable) and then invest the difference. What difference? The premium for level term will run as much as 70% less than the above mentioned types, and you should put yourself in a forced savings program for that saved amount.

A HOME RUN

One interesting approach is to open an IRA on a monthly checking draw for the amount you save and have it sent to a mutual fund with a long, good, track record. I have reviewed many life policies, and I have never seen one that would beat buying term and investing the premium savings in an IRA in a 20% average annual return mutual fund. Be wary of life insurance agents. The commissions are higher on universal life and whole life than on term and for obvious reasons, the company makes more profit on those products.

THE WORST

There is one other type of insurance that we buy that should be discussed here. Credit life or Mortgage life insurance. The purpose of this insurance is to pay off your mortgage or a particular loan if you die. When you bought that stereo on 90 days same as cash, didn't pay it off in 90 days, and converted the loan to payments you were probably sold credit life. Credit life is the most expensive horrible life insurance there is short of having no insurance. A lender may require you to have life insurance adequate to pay off the loan in the event of your death, but he cannot require you buy it from him, so don't. Finance companies make almost as much on insurance premiums as on interest and the managers are often paid bonuses for selling you the overpriced garbage. Mortgage life is not quite as high, but you can usually buy a level term policy of the same face amount for less than half the cost of Mortgage life insurance. Simple rule, do not buy insurance from a lender.

JUST KISS THE MONEY

You may be thinking that I am a some sort of doom-sayer or that I never had a positive thought in my life. Well, it is not that grim. I am simply stating the facts on these investments and insurance products. Very gradually we have let different changes in financial philosophy creep into our lives. We have got to quit being enamored by the shear complexity of these horrible investments. Please use the KEEP IT SIMPLE STUPID rule of investment. Simple is better, and I know that sounds unAmerican, but just consider the common sense of it. Never invest in anything you do not understand thoroughly, I mean upside down, frontward, and backward. If you cannot explain it to someone else, don't buy it or invest in it. NEVER invest in anything you do not thoroughly understand, (WARNING: sexist joke ahead) except possibly a wife.

PEACE PUPPIES

1) Avoid "Stuffitis"-The Worship of "Stuff"
2) Plant Seeds-Give Money Away To Worthy Causes
3) Develop Your Own "Power Over Purchase"
4) Find What You Are Naturally Gifted At, Enjoy Your
   Work, And Work Hard
5) Live Substantially Below Your Income
6) Sacrifice Now So You Can Have Peace Later
7) You Can Always Spend More Than You Can Make
8) You Must Save Money (The Power Of Compound
   Interest)
9) Learn Basic Negotiating Skills For Great Buys
10) Learn Where To Find Great Buys(The Treasure Hunt)
11) You Must Have Patience To Get Great Buys
12) The Borrower Is The Servant To The Lender,
   Beware!!
13) Use The "Keep It Simple Stupid" Rule Of Investing

CHAPTER TWELVE

FAMILIES AND FUNDS

Money is a major part of family dynamics. It plays more of a major part than most of us want to admit. I have observed that the families who have good control of their money seem, by that same strength of character, to have strong families that raise children who are contributors to society. That is not to say that good families do not have financial problems, because many of us have, but the same strong character qualities that raise and run strong families protect people from a lifetime of financial problems.

THE FAMILY DYNAMIC

Money, how it is handled, and how it is managed plays an intense role in the dynamic of the family. It contains this dynamic, not because of its intrinsic value, but because the flow of money represents the value system which that family is operating under. In husband and wife relationships or relationships with children (teenage and above) the flow, control, and management of money is a real point of pressure.

VIVA LA DIFFERENCE

Most men draw much of their self-esteem or ego satisfaction from a sense of accomplishment in their chosen career, and in America we seem to keep score on the success of the career by dollar amounts. So money, the lack of it, or the poor management of it, can have an empowering or devastating effect on the husband.

The number of men who commit suicide due to financial collapse many times outnumbers women's suicides for the same reason. After observing several hundred cases, I have drawn these generalized conclusions, but everyone does react somewhat differently. Women derive something different from the way money is managed in the household. They draw security and peace from the proper handling of household finances. If the money is managed poorly and there is a constant stress, the wife will tend to feel insecure. Both sexes feel intense pressure on this subject. However, they react differently and will therefore make different types of mistakes.

Only an ostrich, with his head buried, would say that money is not a major issue in family life as we close this century. Most all divorces list financial problems as the reason, if not one of the major reasons, that we have "irreconcilable differences."

Most husband and wife teams have such a limited knowledge of basic household financial principles that they are afraid to even discuss the issue.

CAN WE TALK?

A prominent physiologist interviewed recently said, "Discussing money is the taboo of today. Couples are more likely to openly and explicitly discuss sex than to discuss money."

Sickness is allowed, but a sick financial situation is not, perhaps because we feel we are responsible. But why is it that we all pity, and will do anything in the world for poor Uncle Harry who has lung cancer after smoking three packs of cigarettes a day for 30 years, and then we look down our noses at Uncle Joe if he goes bankrupt from mismanagement? Both should be supported, loved, and prayed for, even though both clearly brought it on themselves. Our family members with financial problems do not need to be outcasts, but neither do they need us to make a living for them. You can and should assist with basic necessities through hard times, if you are able, but then lead them to knowledge of proper management, not prolonged support. "Give them a fish and they eat for a day. Teach them to fish and they eat for a lifetime."

We all visualize retiring with peace and security while sitting on the front porch rocking away our twilight years. This scene will not take place unless we do two things in the financial arena. One, learn to handle money, and two, teach our children to handle money. We have lost the art of teaching our children the basic principles outlined in this book and others like it.

JEWISH WISDOM

Larry Burkett, leading financial author, tells of the Jewish tradition of retirement in Biblical times:

"At retirement age (today age 65) the oldest male child (oldest female if there were no sons) was given all the father's assets. Great deal right? No, not so great, because with the transfer of all the parents wealth came the responsibility of caring for the parents and any unmarried sisters until their death."

Now think with me just a minute. If I know I am going to have to depend on my oldest son to provide a good lifestyle, food, shelter, and clothing during my twilight years and if he doesn't I will go hungry. Guess who is going to be a financial genius by the time I get through with him? In my case he WOULD learn to handle money, I promise!!! I think we should learn financial principles, then pass them on to our children as if our life depended on it.

TEACH THE CHILDREN

Teach the children!! Start young. We started with our children at age three. They have certain work responsibilities like cleaning up toys and keeping their rooms clean for which they are paid a small commission. Did you know a five year old can clean the dinner table? The commission teaches the value of work. Work get paid. Do not work, do not get paid, and it is enforced.

We then have the opportunity to use the commissions to teach other lessons. Like giving to good causes, saving, shopping, not spending all you make, the thrill of working -earning-saving-shopping-and finally buying the item you set out for. What a confidence builder for a five year old! What kind of self esteem do you think teenagers would have if they were raised in household that taught this? Children learn by hands on implementation, their hands. Children do not learn to handle money by discussion of vague concepts, they learn by experience. Please notice I did not call the money earned an "allowance", but a commission. We are not teaching our children that they are someone who needs to be made allowance for.

BUT YOU GOTTA LIVE IT

Also, teach your children by your example. When my oldest child was very young she made a little plaque in pre-school which sits on my desk as a reminder. The brave teacher set their little feet in wet paint, then carefully on the plaque. Then they wrote above the footprints: "I am following in your footsteps." Children learn by example.

A real technique to saving on expenses is to train the family early to do things as a team. If the house needs painting, while it is much more trouble than hiring the work done, consider doing it as a family project. The children learn to give to the common good of the family, though the actual work may not have anything to do directly with them at that moment in time. If the family can learn to pull together on work projects, values like unselfishness and hard work are instilled, and you will save money on that project.

THE OLD DAYS

What if a family, that had three married children, were to pitch in together on very large projects. Each young couple, after saving for a few years, could quite possibly pay cash for a house because they all help build each other's homes like the old fashioned barn raisings. In years past in rural America whole communities would gather for a day and build a barn for a neighbor. This seemingly unselfish act worked, because each knew that when his turn came everyone would help him, too. A family raised doing projects together, could furnish the labor on a house, and with no profit, housing costs could be cut by more than 50 percent. This teamwork can start on something as simple as yard work, or doing work for the church, or a widow. The time spent together will build memories, save money, and develop character in your family.

THINK LONG TERM

Let's look at some more long term strategies for the family and money. Most parents are concerned about funding their children's education. Everyone knows you should save for your child's education. But how important is it to save? Most couples start getting serious about college savings when the child gets to junior high school, but by then it is almost too late. Remember the magic of compound interest over time. TIME is one of the key words here. If you wait until the child is 12 to start saving it won't work.

Suppose you want to have $40,000 saved by the time your child starts college. For our example we will use the long term rate of 16%, which is very attainable, as we have discussed. At age 12 (6 years to go) you need to invest $16,417 one time or get prepared to dish out $334 per month. Those figures are simply not real for most families. But, what if you start at age one (17 years to go)? You would need to put $3,208 in that same account ONE time, or you could put $38 per month aside, and still get the same result. YOU MUST START EARLY.

ANOTHER WEIRD IDEA

What if you decided as a result of the pain that you've experienced and the knowledge you have gained that you would like to have your children start married life debt-free? Because you have equipped them with knowledge they could maintain their life debt-free. What if the first few years of marriage for your children were not plagued by financial pressures along with all the natural difficult adjustments? Do you think that their marriages might have a better chance of survival? I think, yes. So I suggest a college fund and a "debt-free fund." I want my children to pay cash for their first home and get a great deal at a foreclosure. I want their cars to be excellent buys, paid for with cash, at the repo lot. I want them to have the knowledge to maintain and appreciate their legacy. As proof they have, they will immediately begin saving the equivalent of a house payment and a car payment to insure that my grandchildren will also start their adult lives debt-free.

With some planning by me TODAY, and some dramatic lessons taught to my children, my marriage could be the last one in my family tree to experience the stress of financial problems brought on by borrowing. Double or triple your college fund for a "debt-free fund", if you start early it is easy!!

The values and practices that operate in the family dynamic today are the ones that will be practiced tomorrow by the following generations only magnified. If you make a firm decision to add discipline and knowledge to your financial life, and then to firmly instill those values in your children, you have the ability to not only begin changing your life today, but more importantly that of all your family after you.

PEACE PUPPIES

1) Avoid "Stuffitis"-The Worship of "Stuff"

2) Plant Seeds-Give Money Away To Worthy Causes

3) Develop Your Own "Power Over Purchase"

4) Find What You Are Naturally Gifted At, Enjoy Your Work, And Work Hard

5) Live Substantially Below Your Income

6) Sacrifice Now So You Can Have Peace Later

7) You Can Always Spend More Than You Can Make

8) You Must Save Money (The Power Of Compound Interest)

9) Learn Basic Negotiating Skills For Great Buys

10) Learn Where To Find Great Buys(The Treasure Hunt)

11) You Must Have Patience To Get Great Buys

12) The Borrower Is The Servant To The Lender, Beware!!

13) Use The "Keep It Simple Stupid" Rule Of Investing

14) Communicate With Your Spouse About Money

15) Teach The Children!!!

CHAPTER THIRTEEN

CAREFULLY CONSIDER COUNSEL

It is time for all of us to grow up enough to quit thinking that we are the "John Wayne" of our finances. You do not have the corner on all the knowledge of the financial world, nor do I. You cannot ride in on your white horse make snap decisions, implement quickie strategies, and still be ready for the next commercial. Our financial lives are more complex in this time than the consumer, or even the professional investor, can fully comprehend on his own. The man, woman, or couple who make significant financial decisions, without first the careful consideration of outside counsel, are destined for pain and heartache.

HOME IS WHERE THE HEART IS

The very first place counsel should be sought is in your home. Yes, your spouse does have a brain and one that may even work better than yours. The traditional sexist relationship where the wife is not involved in matters of money is not only short-sighted, it is just plain dumb. On the other hand the "modern" woman who allows her husband to completely dump all the finances on her is not only being mistreated, she is missing out on basic opportunities of communication in a good marriage.

Strong statements? Well how is it supposed to be? I normally see that one of the two partners is naturally more adept at handling numbers and keeping up with budgets, and that person should do so. It doesn't matter whether this person is the man or the woman. That person should keep the records, but not make all the decisions.

WE GOTTA TALK

As you might have guessed, in my home I am the one who likes numbers, but before I write the monthly bills or make a purchase of significance I have learned to review at least a summary with my wife. This review forces me to look carefully at priorities, because I have to show her. More importantly, it gives us a point of clear communication on where we are and where we are going (no surprises).

You would be surprised at the number of men who have been in my office who hated to keep the checkbook, but thought it was their duty to do so as head of the household. The result was inefficient record-keeping and management by someone operating outside his natural gifts. The man, who turns the record-keeping over to his gifted wife, and does not surrender all the decision making, is wise and has lost no footing. But sometimes we carry ideas too far. I have seen couples who figured out that in their particular marriage the wife was the "numbers" person, but then not only were the record-keeping duties given to her, but all of the financial decisions. Any time one member of a marriage is making most or all of the financial decisions without the consultation of the other the basic communication of the marriage has something lacking, and they are usually headed for financial problems. Remember, common sense, two heads are better than one.

IT IS COMMON SENSE

Money has such a dynamic to it that it plays a role in our relationships many times even when we don't realize it. You might say, "I am not controlled by money." You may be one of those people for whom money has very little impact, but to assume that it does not play a significant role in many of your relationships and even in your marriage is naive'. You will benefit if you learn to communicate with your spouse and take counsel from him or her. I know it is hard to take the time and even hard to break down some walls of pride to openly discuss money at home. If you don't, you will have some difficult lessons ahead.

A note to men. If you do not draw on all your resources when making decisions you are not wise. Many men in this country still have a "macho" need to completely control all financial matters, and many wives even like it this way. Wrong move. Guys, God gave women a sixth sense called women's intuition which he did not give us. Most women have the ability to come to the right decision even if they totally misunderstand or have not a clue about the data. I am a very logical person so I fought this for years and I can't tell you how much money it cost me and how much I've saved since taking my wife's advice. Women often get the right answer by "feeling" it.

THE WORLD'S GREATEST FINANCIER

Several years ago I found an investment house to buy to fix up for resale and profit. The foundation had collapsed and the house needed major repairs. After carefully figuring my repair costs, including getting bids on the work to be done, I bought the house for $6,200. At that great price, plus the work to be done, I determined that my profit would be over $30,000 on this one deal. I was excited. I had made the deal of deals! My wife has a college degree in a totally separate area than finance and hates numbers and dealing with money matters, so I never used to bother her with my deals, I just brought home the bacon.

I took this sweet woman out to see my "deal", which of course looked awful because work was just beginning. When we drove up in front of the house she said I had gotten a bad deal, she just felt it. For the entire 30-minute ride home I preached to her about her lack of ability to see past the work to be done and about her lack of ability with the basics of business and finance.

I STEPPED IN IT

The repairs to the house and the foundation were completed at the predicted price estimates and I was ready for big profits. One day as we were trying to sell that property I drove up in front and to my horror my new foundation had fallen. We put up another wall, and it fell. As we replaced the foundation the THIRD TIME we discovered a wet weather spring which was running against the front of the home. We were able to redirect the spring, and the foundation stands today, but I ended up LOSING over $25,000 on my great "deal." Never underestimate the power of your spouse's counsel. (P.S. She never said, "I told you so," but I deserved it.)

One more stereotype should be dispelled here while we are on the subject of marriage and money. Larry Burkett in his money management teachings talks about this phenomenon and I must concur. In my experience counseling couples through troubled financial situations, I have not found women to have the over-spending problem. When a woman goes crazy spending she usually redecorates a room or buys some clothes, and the dent is $500 to $1500. But when a man goes crazy he comes home with an elaborate investment of $50,000 in a new Lama breeding technique or buys a third car (his toy that of course he can make a profit on) for $15,000. Not all, but most women, tend to be the ones who watch the household finances with a conservative eye. I think this comes from a maternal instinct to protect the home.

GOOD OLE MOM AND DAD

We should also consider counsel from our parents. In our teenage years we struggle and finally wrench free from what we perceive as bondage to our parents. We are free at last to make our own decisions. Many of us made such a wrenching leap into our so called "adulthood" that even many years later we have trouble coming back to our parents for advice.

Those of us who have not utilized this source of wise counsel have missed many an opportunity to avoid pain, and also we have missed the opportunity of developing rich adult-to-adult relationships with our parents like they should be. It takes an emotionally secure person to seek and seriously consider the counsel of parents. We still hear disrespectful, angry, statements like "old fool." Let me assure you, there are very few OLD fools, because living their lives watching young fools has made them wise.

Proverbs 12:15 "The way of a fool is right in his own eyes, but he who hears counsel is wise."

YOUR PASTOR

You should also seek counsel from your spiritual leader. Your pastor, priest, or whatever title is given to that person who guides and instructs you in spiritual and eternal matters. If you are willing to trust your eternal soul to this person's direction, you should also seek his or her counsel in financial matters. As a Christian I believe God will give my pastor wisdom in matters he might not seem to have access to through his background or education. So I will seek his advice in decisions of importance.

Along the same spiritual lines, my primary counsel is the counsel of God through prayer.

Lastly, seek out the opinions and viewpoints of the "experts." Seek their knowledge through personal discussions and/or reading the many books or publications available on a given subject. Be careful NOT to take advice solely from an expert who makes a sales commission when you follow his "advice." There are many well informed and well meaning brokers who are more than willing to give you their "expert" counsel, but there is an inherent conflict of interest in the way they get paid. Many times the integrity is sterling and the advice proper. Sadly, just as many times it is not.

If your "Financial Planner" wants you to invest in a Hybrid African Beetle Tax Shelter, but your wife and parents think it is not smart, you might take more time to consider the matter. Do not get caught in the "They-don't-understand-intricate-financial-transactions" syndrome, because mother may *really* know best.

The balance of considering and weighing counsel from various sources to come to the proper decision is not an easy task. I have found that weighing the counsel is not normally the problem in people we have met with, but rather that they did not take time to seek ANY counsel. We move too fast. We get "buying fever" and don't want anyone to tell us not to do it, until after the crash. Then we want to know why no one told us not to make that purchase. Just slow down and be careful to seek the counsel of love, experience, and knowledge when making significant financial moves.

PEACE PUPPIES

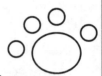

1) Avoid "Stuffitis"-The Worship of "Stuff"
2) Plant Seeds-Give Money Away To Worthy Causes
3) Develop Your Own "Power Over Purchase"
4) Find What You Are Naturally Gifted At, Enjoy Your Work, And Work Hard
5) Live Substantially Below Your Income
6) Sacrifice Now So You Can Have Peace Later
7) You Can Always Spend More Than You Can Make
8) You Must Save Money (The Power Of Compound Interest)
9) Learn Basic Negotiating Skills For Great Buys
10) Learn Where To Find Great Buys(The Treasure Hunt)
11) You Must Have Patience To Get Great Buys
12) The Borrower Is The Servant To The Lender, Beware!!
13) Use The "Keep It Simple Stupid" Rule Of Investing
14) Communicate With Your Spouse About Money
15) Teach The Children!!!
16) Listen To Your Spouse's Counsel (Women's Intuition)
17) There Are Few "Old" Fools, Seek Experienced Counsel

CHAPTER FOURTEEN

WHY WRITTEN ???

What would you say the chances of success are for a business that keeps no records and does no forecasting of income or expenses? I would say the chances for failure are very high and the chances of success slim to none. The Small Business Administration says that the number one reason for small business failure is poor record-keeping.

IS YOUR BUSINESS GOING BROKE?

This fact comes as no surprise to most of us, and yet 90 to 95% of American households operate without a detailed accurate written outline of income and expenses. They have only a slight clue as to what it takes to keep their household "in business" every month. Not one in 150 people that I have counseled for financial woes had an accurate list of obligations and expenses when they first come to me. No one does it!! To use some overworked expressions: By failing to plan we are planning to fail and so there is always too much month left at the end of the money.

MORE DIRTY WORDS

I have bad news. Everyone needs a written budget. When I say this I hear things like, "A budget, oh no, not me I am a free spirit!!" or "Not a budget for me - things are pretty well under control" or "Only nerds do written budgets, you know the guys with the calculator on their belt who don't have anything better to do on Saturday night." Wrong, Wrong, Wrong.

The word budget is a derivative of the French word *bougette*, a form of *bouge*, which is a small leather purse. When we discuss budgets we think of small amounts, stingy, a dark room where we can't get out. With these perceptions it is no wonder we don't monthly plan our cash flow.

We have developed this view of budgeting as if it is a little known form of torture. A correctly prepared budget is not a form of torture, nor is it so time consuming that you can't have Saturday night out. On the contrary, a proper, simple, written plan will actually give you more free time and money with which to enjoy it.

THE AMAZING GROWING MONEY

I counseled a young single man recently, who after we put some simple budgeting measures and plans in place, called to say it was as if his money had grown, as if money was coming in from nowhere. Okay, if you don't want to call it a budget call it a "cash flow plan", maybe that won't seem so harsh. But we must implement some written strategies for forecasting and controlling our money.

Sitting down, and developing a budget or cash flow plan doesn't sound like much fun does it? Does going on to Europe, Cancun SCUBA diving, or Aspen snow skiing and coming home to face no debt or credit card bills sound like fun? That is what a proper plan will do for you because you can begin planning that debt-free vacation as a part of your plan today. If you are a free spirit and want to have more freedom, time to write, or paint then plan financially to attain that status. But until you plan you will never reach "free spirit" status financially because "unexpected" bills will always clip your wings.

IT IS NOT A WHIP

A cash flow plan is not a method of manipulation for one family member over another. I know in some households the term is used in such a negative connotation that most people would rather have termites in the house than a written budget. But just keep in mind that approach is a misuse of the idea. It is the reflection of the character of the manipulator, not of the concept of cash flow control.

A good written plan comes from the communication and input of all family members and then is implemented by the joint efforts of all family members. I keep saying simple plan, because a good plan should not be time consuming. Most experts agree an accurate plan can be derived in two to six hours the first time and should be able to be maintained in less that 15 minutes a week. If you are spending more time than that on the average household budget it is because you are leaving things out and thereby putting stress on the plan, or you have overcomplicated it. You should KISS your budget too.

I SAID WRITTEN

Sometimes I hear, "Well I kinda sorta know where my money is, ya know, I know what it is going to, ya know, I do my planning in my mind, ya know." Having a *WRITTEN* plan is absolutely necessary. Have you ever had a problem you were dying to discuss to get someone's answer to? And when you sat down and began telling him the whole situation you were able to answer the question for yourself? So you answer your own question, leaving the other person sitting there wondering why you asked.

There is a reason this has happened to each of us. The information that is scrambled in your brain has to be categorized, summarized, and organized very quickly to verbalize it. This clarification of information which has occurred for the sake of communication, clears your mind and allows you to answer your own question. Then we say something like, "I just needed someone to bounce it off of."

THE CLEARING OF A FOG

Developing a written plan does the exact same thing for your finances. To accurately develop a plan you have to gather, organize, categorize, and analyze information about your money situation. We will NEVER do this unless we sit down to put our situation on paper. As you begin to organize this information you will be amazed that answers to problems will appear easily.

The accurate picture is just the first benefit. Something mystical happens when we commit something personal to writing. We somehow begin to live out our plans. I am not saying that if you do a written plan you will fall into a trance and automatically carry out the very last detail. Clarifying your goals and aspirations, then facing financial realities changes the way you see your situation. When you see what must be done you will begin to move in that direction as a matter of course. Honestly, the ONLY way most of you will ever see that exotic vacation, you probably deserve, is to have a written plan that controls household income and expenses to enable you to begin saving for it.

A- B- C   1- 2 - 3

Are you wondering how to get to this magical place known as "cash flow plan land?" I promise not to leave you here with just vague suggestions. I will present three specific steps you can follow to develop a written cash flow plan. Easy-to-follow instructions and forms are in the Appendix A to help you develop your written plan. It is as easy as A - B - C.

Step A
Keep Your Checkbook Properly
Recorded And Balanced

Sounds so simple, doesn't it? Then why do so few people do it? Bank officers tell horror stories of people who bring in checking accounts so far out of balance the only thing that can be done is close them and start over with a new account. The math involved in keeping and balancing a checkbook is basic addition and subtraction, and yet most of us have experienced the frustration of an account that won't balance. Why? Because of several factors.

RUSH RUSH RUSH

Do you ever get in a hurry and forget to record the proper amount? Burkett says and we all have experienced being in this long line of impatient people at the grocery store, and we are scared to death that someone might have to wait 30 seconds longer while I record my check. Then when I get home I can't remember the right amount. I know, I have done it. Or sometimes we record the checks, but never bring the balance forward. Maybe we don't want to know how low it is. I have seen many people who don't reconcile or balance their checkbooks for six months at a time. We must begin keeping an accurate checkbook.

If you have trouble recording your checks, try using duplicate checks. Most banks sell a NCR paper or carbon check, which automatically records your check as you write it. You still have to carry your balance forward and reconcile your checkbook to the statement each month. I use a similar system for my business accounts.

DON'T DO THIS

I know a financial counselor who was trying to help a client get his checkbook back in balance. The client had a history of bouncing checks. As the counselor went through the checkbook he found neat and precise recording with balances carried forward. He couldn't find these persistent errors. As he looked he saw $28 for gas, $92 for electricity, $359 for car payment, $128 for clothes, and $78 for ESP. After reviewing the checkbook carefully he simply could not find the errors, so he called in the client and told him. The counselor said, "My only question is what is ESP?" and the client answered, "Error Some Place." This is not the way you balance a checkbook. The ESP method does not work.

BUDGET BUSTER

Beware of automatic teller machine cards. These cards are a wonderful convenience, and we use ours for emergency cash withdrawals, but as a cash management tool they are a record-keeping nightmare. Even people who do a good job recording their checks forget to post the automatic teller withdrawals. Haven't you seen all the little computer receipts left at the machine? That tells you most people don't record those transactions. It is best to deal in cash. Some wonderful cash handling techniques will follow that will protect you from "budget busters" or impulse decisions at the automatic teller machine.

Step B
Write Out The Details

In Appendix A you will find simple forms that will help you to lay out an accurate monthly cash flow plan. If you will simply take the time to fill out the forms, you will be well on your way to getting control.

Some categories on the forms require a little explanation. First, the "Blow" category. Plan to blow, waste, or not account for some portion of your money. If you do not plan this you will do it anyway. The problem isn't that we do not have this category now, the problem is that most people's blow category is their entire plan. A regimented plan that is too tight is not realistic. If you do not allow some cushion in your plan you will fail. Then you will say that plans do not work for you. Wrong.

A good plan lives and moves - is dynamic - changes as your life changes. You will need to do a detailed review every three to four months to make adjustments. You may have budgeted too little for some areas, and be strained, you will need to adjust. Some areas you will have budgeted too much, and have a surplus, you need to adjust. If you have lived on an ill-prepared budget, or no budget at all, it will take you a few minor adjustments to get the plan to a realistic level. The plan is not to complicate your life, on the contrary, when you begin to know where your cash is flowing it will make life easier. You cannot possibly realize you are spending too much on a category, if you don't track your spending.

IMPORTANT IMPORTANT.

If you do nothing else I have suggested, this little section will change your finances dramatically. Numerous clients have testified of the power of this simple control mechanism. Many writers have recommended the use of this technique, and through practical experience I have found it to be overwhelmingly powerful in the average consumer household. It is the time-honored "envelope system" of cash management, a budgeting system recommended by most good financial counselors.

Items you use a credit card or a check for, out of supposed convenience, will likely become budget busters if you continue. For example, suppose you budget $600 per month for groceries, eating out, and prescription drugs. Most people write a check at the grocery store, use a credit card at the restaurant, then another check at the grocery store, and at the end of the month they look back and realize it all adds up to $700. They went over their budget by $100. Unless you keep very careful and cumbersome records throughout the month (and most of you won't) you will usually bust your budget.

SIMPLE AS PIE

Implementing the envelope system is simple. If you get paid twice a month, write a check for three hundred dollars to yourself for food on each payday. Then cash the check, and put the $300 cash in an envelope, which you mark "FOOD." As you need to buy food, take the money from that envelope and from nowhere else. This does several things for you. It provides you with instantaneous cash management in that you will almost never spend more than allotted. The only way to spend more is to get the money from somewhere else. If you are thinking it has been a hard week and you "deserve" to go out to eat on Friday night, simply pull out the "FOOD" envelope. Look into the envelope to see if you can afford to do what you need to do. You don't need a complicated bookkeeping system to track your budget. Just look in the envelope.

EMOTION IS A GREAT MANAGER

Remember the power of cash as an emotional negotiating tool? Now you will see the power of that emotion work on you to help you lessen your spending. It is much easier to sign a check or a credit card receipt than it is to lay down cold hard cash to pay for something. When you spend cash it hurts a little bit, so you will end up spending less. When we started using the envelope system for food our expenditures on food dropped by over $100 per month. We were going out more than we needed. We do not punish ourselves, we simply manage ourselves. I still enjoy taking my wife out on a date to a nice restaurant, but we just do it by plan now. If we want a romantic dinner on impulse we just check to see if we get cheap romantic or expensive romantic. Romance is more romantic with financial freedom.

You can also use the envelope system for other areas as well. I use it for gasoline and other categories shown on the form system. The categories I suggest the envelope system for have a star by them on the forms. I have also suggested the envelope system to use in reverse on small savings items. If you set aside $200 per month for car repairs, maintenance, and tires, you can either deposit that into a savings account or simply keep the money in an envelope. Then as you need to do repairs the money is right there, and you can manage the repairs. If you are afraid to have much cash around the house, I suggest using a categorized savings program which we will discuss in the forms section.

ESTATE PLANNING, A MUST

The last area to address in laying out the details is the paperwork of estate planning. Estate planning from a tax perspective or legal perspective can be very complicated, and you should seek competent legal counsel. I will not address details here. What we do need to talk about is the common sense side of it, though. If you do not have a current will, get one now. It is a biological, statistical, and spiritual fact you are going to die. Most of us have avoided completing this little task of writing a will because we think it is morbid, or we are superstitious enough to believe that preparing a will hastens our death. Silly. If you want to control your estate and be responsible to your family you need to have a current will.

Once you have a will, you should address the major areas of insurance, life, health, disability, auto, and homeowners. Carefully review your coverages and fill in any gaps in coverage. Periodically update your entire insurance program.

Next, designate a specific place where all the details of your estate are kept. I use a certain drawer in my desk that has a file on each area. My wife knows that if something happens to me, everything she needs to know about our affairs is in that drawer. In addition to that write out detailed instructions to your spouse regarding each area. The last thing a spouse needs to think about in the middle of a crisis is where all the insurance policies are, where the account numbers on savings programs are, and/or where the will is. Do some simple organization and preparation as a practical estate planning tool. Your attention now can prevent confusion or costly mistakes later.

Step C
Commit To Your Plan For 90 Days

You have tried living your life the other way all this time, so give these suggestions a real opportunity to take hold. A one-week trial run and the "I can't do it" is not a fair or proper analysis. I am asking you to commit to trying a written plan for 90 days. I mean COMMIT. Do not let anything pull you away, if you do not set out with a firm commitment, you will probably give up within the first three weeks. If you will stay with it 90 days, I promise you will work the kinks out, and your financial life will never be the same. You will have formed a positive new habit. Successful people know the value of discipline in their lives. I believe committing to your plan for 90 days will change your life. Ninety days would be less than 1% of your life, and if you have read this far, you have got what it takes to do it. So do it!!

JUST DO IT

We have talked about something that few American households do, development of an accurate, dynamic, written cash management plan. I cannot stress the importance of this enough as a method for getting control of your finances. Don't let a written budget become a huge monster in your mind, because it does not have to be overwhelming. Please commit to this for 90 days. I have counseled

Why Written

so many hurting consumers and business people on the brink of bankruptcy, and it makes me ache inside when I know that a simple budget could have saved most of them numerous heartaches. Please try it.

PEACE PUPPIES

1) Avoid "Stuffitis"-The Worship of "Stuff"
2) Plant Seeds-Give Money Away To Worthy Causes
3) Develop Your Own "Power Over Purchase"
4) Find What You Are Naturally Gifted At, Enjoy Your
    Work, And Work Hard
5) Live Substantially Below Your Income
6) Sacrifice Now So You Can Have Peace Later
7) You Can Always Spend More Than You Can Make
8) You Must Save Money (The Power Of Compound
    Interest)
9) Learn Basic Negotiating Skills For Great Buys
10) Learn Where To Find Great Buys(The Treasure Hunt)
11) You Must Have Patience To Get Great Buys
12) The Borrower Is The Servant To The Lender,
    Beware!!
13) Use The "Keep It Simple Stupid" Rule Of Investing
14) Communicate With Your Spouse About Money
15) Teach The Children!!!
16) Listen To Your Spouse's Counsel (Women's Intuition)
17) There Are Few "Old" Fools, Seek Experienced
    Counsel
18) You Must Keep Your Checkbook On A Timely Basis
19) Lay Out The Written Details Of A Cash Management
    Plan
20) Commit To Trying These Principles For 90 Days

CHAPTER FIFTEEN

DO IT DAILY

Consciously prioritize your life everyday. Most of you need to do this very practical exercise in the morning. Yes, I am saying get up 30 minutes earlier. Get up and spend some time in the quiet of the morning assessing where you are and where you want to be. Most of us have grown up in an alarm clock society where we leap out of bed and run through the shower straight to the car where we drink our first cup of coffee and put on our tie or make-up on the way to work, barely making it on time. When I sit in traffic I am amazed at the number of people who are really fairly good drivers using their knees to steer while they have breakfast and get dressed on the way to work.

THINKING CHANGES THINGS

You can not only dramatically affect your financial life by having quiet time early in the morning, but it will affect your career and your spiritual condition positively as well. In days past

America was largely an agricultural society and we kept different hours. My grandfather will still get up from his chair at 8:30 P.M and say, "Honey, we are going to have to go to bed so these folks can go home." He was raised in a household where you got up at sunrise, worked hard physically all day, and then wanted to go to bed early. We do what we really want to do. If you truly want to change certain areas of your life to avoid pain and then prosper, you will have to try new ways of doing things. You have probably had the experience of having an exciting day planned on Saturday, knowing you had to wake up early, and wake up 30 minutes before the alarm clock goes off. It is amazing how your mind and body will cooperate for something you really want to do.

TAKE THE TIME

If you want to have time to consciously prioritize your life daily, you will make the necessary changes in your lifestyle to accommodate that few minutes of serenity each day. Spend your quite time learning from your past by review, looking over where you need to be in five years emotionally, with your family, and your career. This time of reflection will give you time to make adjustments in all these areas of your life.

Search out the spiritual. Your make-up is more than just physical and emotional, it is also spiritual. I spend my time looking to the Lord Jesus Christ daily and weekly in church to strengthen and guide my life. What does this have to do with money? Everything. We are spiritual beings and when you neglect that aspect of your life, you are not running on full power, so all areas of your life will be affected, including money. Yes, Christians have money problems too, but they have an extra ability to survive and prosper in the long run.

As you add a quiet time and grow spiritually the quality of your life will improve, and so will your financial condition. The personal growth and financial growth that these simple little changes in my daily schedule have brought me is immeasurable. My day starts under control and so when the torpedoes hit, and they often do, then I am ready because I'm not alone.

PEACE PUPPIES

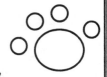

1) Avoid "Stuffitis"-The Worship of "stuff"

2) Plant Seeds-Give Money Away To Worthy Causes

3) Develop Your Own "Power Over Purchase"

4) Find What You Are Naturally Gifted At, Enjoy Your Work, And Work Hard

5) Live Substantially Below Your Income

6) Sacrifice Now So You Can Have Peace Later

7) You Can Always Spend More Than You Can Make

8) You Must Save Money (The Power Of Compound Interest)

9) Learn Basic Negotiating Skills For Great Buys

10) Learn Where To Find Great Buys(The Treasure Hunt)

11) You Must Have Patience To Get Great Buys

12) The Borrower Is The Servant To The Lender, Beware!!

13) Use The "Keep It Simple Stupid" Rule Of Investing

14) Communicate With Your Spouse About Money

15) Teach The Children!!!

16) Listen To Your Spouse's Counsel (Women's Intuition)

17) There Are Few "Old" Fools, Seek Experienced Counsel

18) You Must Keep Your Checkbook On A Timely Basis

19) Lay Out The Written Details Of A Cash Management Plan

20) Commit To Trying These Principles For 90 Days

21) Take Time To Prioritize Your Live Daily

22) Keep Your Spiritual Life Healthy

CHAPTER SIXTEEN

THE END . . . OR JUST THE BEGINNING ??

Well, now it is time. Time for you to decide. Are you a man or a mouse? Are you a woman or a wimp? Are you going to change the way you do things, or are you going to put this book on the shelf to collect dust with all the other self-help books? We human beings resist change, and it takes a conscious and determined effort to make even the slightest changes in our lives.

NOBODY IS PERFECT

I do not do all the things suggested in the previous pages perfectly. But I do continually make myself aware of what needs to be done and do the best I can at each area. Believe me a 25% improvement change in each area will change your life dramatically. It takes time to implement changes in all these areas. It took me some time, but with each change it gets easier. One day you will suddenly realize that you are getting under control! That is the way you eat a whole elephant, one bite at a time. Over time and with a conscious effort I have implemented these principles in my life to where we are up to about the 90% implementation level. Things are really starting to get FUN.

You really do not have a choice, either you will start controlling your money, or it will forever control you. You can do it! Get a tight grip and hold on. You are in for a thrilling ride.

People consider me a strong person with strong opinions, but even I had a hard time getting started and staying on track with making these life changing decisions. These are decisions that call for sacrifice, discipline, and patience. Three tough words.

LESSONS LEARNED

I have been to the top, and then the bottom, and back again financially, and whatever you are facing you can survive. No matter what you gain or lose in material goods you can never have talent and hope taken from you, unless you surrender it. I must tell you as we close that there is no way within my own strength that I could have survived learning these lessons the hard way. Only through the power of Christ who strengthens me was this possible.

We have been discussing "peace" and how to attain financial "peace" at length. The "peace" we have been referring to, in our context, comes from better manipulation of variables outside ourselves.

. . . The Beginning

Through the steps we have outlined you can achieve that type of "peace," but you will never find real "peace" from any amount of manipulation of earthly *"stuff."* The only real "peace" is the "peace that passes all understanding" through Christ. I never found true contentment, "peace," through any method or formula until I found Him.

Learn from the pain and experience of one who has been there and one who has witnessed too many others in their own predicament. You do not have to learn the hard way. Please review these principles as an ongoing guide and use them to change your life!

PEACE PUPPIES

1) *Avoid "Stuffitis"-The Worship of "Stuff"*
2) *Plant Seeds-Give Money Away To Worthy Causes*
3) *Develop Your Own "Power Over Purchase"*
4) *Find What You Are Naturally Gifted At, Enjoy Your Work, And Work Hard*
5) *Live Substantially Below Your Income*
6) *Sacrifice Now So You Can Have Peace Later*
7) *You Can Always Spend More Than You Can Make*
8) *You Must Save Money (The Power Of Compound Interest)*
9) *Learn Basic Negotiating Skills For Great Buys*
10) *Learn Where To Find Great Buys(The Treasure Hunt)*
11) *You Must Have Patience To Get Great Buys*
12) *The Borrower Is The Servant To The Lender, Beware!!*
13) *Use The "Keep It Simple Stupid" Rule Of Investing*
14) *Communicate With Your Spouse About Money*
15) *Teach The Children!!!*
16) *Listen To Your Spouse's Counsel (Women's Intuition)*
17) *There Are Few "Old" Fools, Seek Experienced Counsel*
18) *You Must Keep Your Checkbook On A Timely Basis*
19) *Lay Out The Written Details Of A Cash Management Plan*
20) *Commit To Trying These Principles For 90 Days*
21) *Take Time To Prioritize Your Live Daily*
22) *Keep Your Spiritual Life Healthy*

FINANCIAL MANAGEMENT FORMS

APPENDIX

A

Welcome to the wonderful world of "cash flow management." Filling out these few forms *and* following your new plan *will* change your financial future. The first time you fill out the forms it will be tough and will take a while. But, each time you come back for another look you will get faster and the forms will be easier so don't get discouraged. The length and the amount of detail I am taking you through may seem overwhelming. However, I have found that if you don't have the detail as a track to run on you leave something out. Guess what that does? If you leave items out that you are really spending you will crash your plan and then you will have an excuse to quit, so just bear down and do all the forms completely one time.

After you have filled out the whole set one time you only need to do Sheet 7 or Sheet 8 (whichever is applicable) once per month which should take about 30 minutes per month. Do Sheet 5 over once per quarter, but since you will see only minor changes from one quarter to the next you should only need about one hour per quarter to update. Then update the entire pack once per year or when any large positive or negative financial event occurs (Aunt Ethel leaves you $10,000 in her will).

Once you have made it through this planning process the first time you should be able to manage your finances in 30 minutes per month plus what it takes to write checks and balance your checkbook. Go for it!!

P. S. Be sure you keep your promises on Sheet 1 and share that completed sheet with your spouse if married.

MAJOR COMPONENTS
OF A
HEALTHY FINANCIAL PLAN

	Action Needed	Action Date
Written Cash Flow Plan	_____	_____
Will and/or Estate Plan	_____	_____
Debt Reduction Plan	_____	_____
Emergency Funding	_____	_____
Retirement Funding	_____	_____
College Funding	_____	_____
Charitable Giving	_____	_____
Teach My Children	_____	_____
Life Insurance	_____	_____
Health Insurance	_____	_____
Disability Insurance	_____	_____
Auto Insurance	_____	_____
Homeowners Insurance	_____	_____

I, _____ a responsible adult do hereby swear to take the above stated actions by the above stated dates to financially secure the well being of my family and my self. (Copy to Spouse)

Signed:_____ Date:_____

INCOME SOURCES

SOURCE	AMOUNT	PERIOD / DESCRIBE
Salary 1		
Salary 2		
Salary 3		
Self-Employment		
Interest Income		
Dividend Income		
Royalty Income		
Rents		
Notes		
Alimony		
Child Support		
AFDC		
Unemployment		
Social Security		
Pension		
Annuity		
Disability Income		
Cash Gifts		
Trust Fund		
Other _____		
Other _____		
Other _____		
Other _____		
TOTAL		

CONSUMER EQUITY SHEET

ITEM / DESCRIBE	VALUE	-	DEBT	=	EQUITY
Real Estate _____	_____		_____		_____
Real Estate _____	_____		_____		_____
Car _____	_____		_____		_____
Car _____	_____		_____		_____
Cash On Hand	_____		_____		_____
Checking Account	_____		_____		_____
Checking Account	_____		_____		_____
Savings Account	_____		_____		_____
Savings Account	_____		_____		_____
Money Market Account	_____		_____		_____
Mutual Funds	_____		_____		_____
Retirement Plan	_____		_____		_____
Stocks or Bonds	_____		_____		_____
Cash Value (Insurance)	_____		_____		_____
Household Items	_____		_____		_____
Jewelry	_____		_____		_____
Antiques	_____		_____		_____
Boat	_____		_____		_____
Other _____	_____		_____		_____
Other _____	_____		_____		_____
Other _____	_____		_____		_____
TOTAL	_____		_____		_____

LUMP SUM PAYMENT PLANNING

Payments you make on a NON monthly basis can be budget busters if not planned for. So we are converting them to a monthly basis for you to use on Sheet 5 where you will set money aside monthly to avoid strain or borrowing when these events occur. If an item here is already paid monthly enter NA. If you make a payment quarterly then annualize it for this sheet.

ITEM NEEDED	ANNUAL AMOUNT		MONTHLY AMOUNT
Real Estate Taxes	_____	/ 12 =	_____
Homeowners Ins.	_____	/ 12 =	_____
Home Repairs	_____	/ 12 =	_____
Replace Furniture	_____	/ 12 =	_____
Medical Bills	_____	/ 12 =	_____
Health Insurance	_____	/ 12 =	_____
Life Insurance	_____	/ 12 =	_____
Disability Ins.	_____	/ 12 =	_____
Car Insurance	_____	/ 12 =	_____
Car Repair/Tags	_____	/ 12 =	_____
Replace Car	_____	/ 12 =	_____
Clothing	_____	/ 12 =	_____
Tuition	_____	/ 12 =	_____
Bank Note	_____	/ 12 =	_____
IRS (Self-Empl.)	_____	/ 12 =	_____
Vacation	_____	/ 12 =	_____
Gifts(inc. Christmas)	_____	/ 12 =	_____
Other _____	_____	/ 12 =	_____
Other _____	_____	/ 12 =	_____

SHEET 5   INSTRUCTIONS:

Every dollar of your income should be allocated to some category on this sheet. Money "left over" should be put back into some category even if you make up a new category. You are making the spending decisions ahead of time here. Almost every category (except debt) should have *some* dollar amount in it. Example: If you do not *plan* to replace the furniture, when you do replace it you will cause strain or borrowing, so go ahead and plan now by saving. I have actually had people tell me that they can do without clothing. Oh come ON!! Be careful in your zeal to make the numbers work that you don't substitute the *urgent* for the *important*.

Fill in the amount for each sub-category under "Sub-total" and then the total for each Main category under "Total." As you go through your first month fill in the "Actually Spent" column with your real expenses or the saving you did for that area. If there is a substantial difference something has to give. You will either have to adjust the amount allocated to that area up and another down or you will have to control your spending in that area better.

"%THP" is percentage of take home pay or "What percentage of your total take home pay did you spend on "Housing" as an example. We will then compare your percentages with those on Sheet 6 to determine if you need to look at adjusting your lifestyle.

* beside an item means you should use the "envelope system" described on pages 167-169 for best results.

(1) Emergency Fund should get ALL the savings until 3-6 months of income is saved.

Note: Savings should be increased as you get closer to being debt free.

Hint: By saving for Christmas and other gifts early you can get great buys and give better gifts for the same money spent.

MONTHLY CASH FLOW PLAN

ITEM	BUDGETED Sub Total	TOTAL	Actually SPENT	% of THP
CHARITABLE GIFTS		_____	_____	_____
SAVING				
Emergency Fund(1)	_____		_____	
Retirement Fund	_____		_____	
College Fund	_____	_____	_____	_____
HOUSING				
First Mortgage	_____		_____	
Second Mortgage	_____		_____	
Real Estate Taxes	_____		_____	
Homeowners Ins.	_____		_____	
Repairs or Mn. Fee	_____		_____	
Replace Furniture	_____		_____	
Other _____	_____	_____	_____	_____
UTILITIES				
Electricity	_____		_____	
Water	_____		_____	
Gas	_____		_____	
Phone	_____		_____	
Trash	_____		_____	
Cable	_____	_____	_____	_____
*FOOD				
*Grocery	_____		_____	
*Restaurants	_____	_____	_____	_____
TRANSPORTATION				
Car Payment	_____		_____	
Car Payment	_____		_____	
*Gas and Oil	_____		_____	
*Repairs and Tires	_____		_____	
Car Insurance	_____		_____	
License and Taxes	_____		_____	
Car Replacement	_____	_____	_____	
PAGE 1 TOTAL		_____	_____	

ITEM	BUDGETED Sub Total	TOTAL	Actually SPENT	% of THP
*CLOTHING				
*Children	_____		_____	
*Adults	_____		_____	
*Cleaning/Laundry	_____	_____	_____	_____
MEDICAL/HEALTH				
Disability Insurance	_____		_____	
Health Insurance	_____		_____	
Doctor Bills	_____		_____	
Dentist	_____		_____	
Optometrist	_____		_____	
Drugs	_____	_____	_____	_____
PERSONAL				
Life Insurance	_____		_____	
Child Care	_____		_____	
*Baby Sitter	_____		_____	
*Toiletries	_____		_____	
*Cosmetics	_____		_____	
*Hair Care	_____		_____	
Education/Adult	_____		_____	
School Tuition	_____		_____	
School Supplies	_____		_____	
Child Support	_____		_____	
Alimony	_____		_____	
Subscriptions	_____		_____	
Organization Dues	_____		_____	
Gifts (inc. Christmas)	_____		_____	
Miscellaneous	_____		_____	
*BLOW $$	_____	_____	_____	_____
PAGE 2 TOTAL		_____	_____	

ITEM	BUDGETED Sub Total	TOTAL	Actually SPENT	% of THP
RECREATION				
*Entertainment	_____		_____	
Vacation	_____	_____	_____	_____
DEBTS (Hopefully -0-)				
Visa 1	_____		_____	
Visa 2	_____		_____	
MasterCard 1	_____		_____	
MasterCard 2	_____		_____	
American Express	_____		_____	
DiscoverCard	_____		_____	
Gas Card 1	_____		_____	
Gas Card 2	_____		_____	
Dept. Store Card 1	_____		_____	
Dept. Store Card 2	_____		_____	
Finance Co. 1	_____		_____	
Finance Co. 2	_____		_____	
Credit Line	_____		_____	
Student Loan 1	_____		_____	
Student Loan 2	_____		_____	
Other _____	_____	_____	_____	
Other _____	_____	_____	_____	
Other _____	_____	_____	_____	
Other _____	_____	_____	_____	
Other _____	_____	_____	_____	_____
PAGE 3 TOTAL		_____	_____	
PAGE 2 TOTAL		_____	_____	
PAGE 1 TOTAL		_____	_____	
GRAND TOTAL		_____	_____	
-TOTAL INCOME		_____		
ZERO		ZERO		

RECOMMENDED PERCENTAGES

I have used a compilation of several sources and my own experience to derive the "suggested" percentage guidelines. However, these are only recommended percentages and will change dramatically if you have a very high or very low income. For instance if you have a very low income your necessities percentages will be over. If you have a high income your necessities will be a lower percentage of income and hopefully savings (not debt) will be higher than recommended .

ITEM	ACTUAL %	RECOMMENDED %
CHARITABLE GIFTS		10-15%
SAVING		5-10%
HOUSING		25-35%
UTILITIES		5-10%
FOOD		5-15%
TRANSPORTATION		10-15%
CLOTHING		2-7%
MEDICAL/HEALTH		5-10%
PERSONAL		5-10%
RECREATION		5-10%
DEBTS		5-10%

SHEET 7   INSTRUCTIONS:

This Sheet is where all your work thus far starts giving you some peace. You will implement Sheet 5 information from theory into your life by using Sheet 7. Note: If you have an irregular income, like self-employment or commissions, then use Sheet 8 instead, after reviewing Sheet 7.

There are 4 columns to distribute as many as 4 different incomes within one month. Each column is one pay period. If you are a one income household and you get paid 2 times per month then you will only use two columns. If both of you work and one is paid weekly and the other every two weeks add the two checks together on the weeks you both get a check while just using the one check on the other two. So date the pay period columns then enter the income for that period below. As you allocate your check to an item put the remaining balance to the right of the slash. Income for period 3-1 in our example is $1,000 and we are allocating $100 to Charitable Giving leaving $900 to the right of the slash in that same column. Some bills will come out of each check and some only certain checks. As an example you may take Car gas out of every check, but pay the electric bill from period 2. You already pay some bills or payments out of certain checks, only now you pay **all** things from certain checks.

The whole point to this sheet, which is the culmination of all your monthly planning, is to allocate or "spend" your whole check before you get it. I don't care where you allocate your money, but allocate all of it before you get your check. Now all the tense, crisis like symptoms have been removed because you planned. No more management by crisis or impulse. Those who want to be impulsive just allocate more to the Blow category at least you are now doing it on purpose and not by default. Your last blank that you make an entry in should have a 0 to the right of the slash, showing you allocated your whole check.

ALLOCATED SPENDING PLAN

PAY PERIOD:	3-1			
ITEM				
INCOME	$1000			
CHARITABLE GIFTS	100/900	/	/	/
SAVING				
Emergency Fund(1)	50/850	/	/	/
Retirement Fund	/	/	/	/
College Fund	/	/	/	/
HOUSING				
First Mortgage	725/125	/	/	/

ALLOCATED SPENDING PLAN

PAY PERIOD: ___ ___ ___ ___

ITEM

INCOME ___ ___ ___ ___

CHARITABLE GIFTS __/__ __/__ __/__ __/·__

SAVING
  Emergency Fund(1) __/__ __/__ __/__ __/__
  Retirement Fund __/__ __/__ __/__ __/__
  College Fund __/__ __/__ __/__ __/__

HOUSING
  First Mortgage __/__ __/__ __/__ __/__
  Second Mortgage __/__ __/__ __/__ __/__
  Real Estate Taxes __/__ __/__ __/__ __/__
  Homeowners Ins. __/__ __/__ __/__ __/__
  Repairs or Mn. Fees __/__ __/__ __/__ __/__
  Replace Furniture __/__ __/__ __/__ __/__
  Other _____ __/__ __/__ __/__ __/__

UTILITIES
  Electricity __/__ __/__ __/__ __/__
  Water __/__ __/__ __/__ __/__
  Gas __/__ __/__ __/__ __/__
  Phone __/__ __/__ __/__ __/__
  Trash __/__ __/__ __/__ __/__
  Cable __/__ __/__ __/__ __/__

*FOOD
  *Grocery __/__ __/__ __/__ __/__
  *Restaurants __/__ __/__ __/__ __/__

TRANSPORTATION
  Car Payment __/__ __/__ __/__ __/__
  Car Payment __/__ __/__ __/__ __/__
  *Gas and Oil __/__ __/__ __/__ __/__
  *Repairs and Tires __/__ __/__ __/__ __/__
  Car Insurance __/__ __/__ __/__ __/__
  License and Taxes __/__ __/__ __/__ __/__
  Car Replacement __/__ __/__ __/__ __/__

*CLOTHING
  *Children   ___/___ ___/___ ___/___ ___/___
  *Adults   ___/___ ___/___ ___/___ ___/___
  *Cleaning/Laundry ___/___ ___/___ ___/___ ___/___

MEDICAL/HEALTH
  Disability Insurance ___/___ ___/___ ___/___ ___/___
  Health Insurance ___/___ ___/___ ___/___ ___/___
  Doctor Bills   ___/___ ___/___ ___/___ ___/___
  Dentist   ___/___ ___/___ ___/___ ___/___
  Optometrist   ___/___ ___/___ ___/___ ___/___
  Drugs   ___/___ ___/___ ___/___ ___/___

PERSONAL
  Life Insurance   ___/___ ___/___ ___/___ ___/___
  Child Care   ___/___ ___/___ ___/___ ___/___
  *Baby Sitter   ___/___ ___/___ ___/___ ___/___
  *Toiletries   ___/___ ___/___ ___/___ ___/___
  *Cosmetics   ___/___ ___/___ ___/___ ___/___
  *Hair Care   ___/___ ___/___ ___/___ ___/___
  Education/Adult   ___/___ ___/___ ___/___ ___/___
  School Tuition   ___/___ ___/___ ___/___ ___/___
  School Supplies   ___/___ ___/___ ___/___ ___/___
  Child Support   ___/___ ___/___ ___/___ ___/___
  Alimony   ___/___ ___/___ ___/___ ___/___
  Subscriptions   ___/___ ___/___ ___/___ ___/___
  Organization Dues ___/___ ___/___ ___/___ ___/___
  Gifts (inc. Christmas)___/___ ___/___ ___/___ ___/___
  Miscellaneous   ___/___ ___/___ ___/___ ___/___
  *BLOW $$ ___/___ ___/___ ___/___ ___/___

RECREATION
  *Entertainment __/__ __/__ __/__ __/__
  Vacation __/__ __/__ __/__ __/__

DEBTS (Hopefully -0-)
  Visa 1 __/__ __/__ __/__ __/__
  Visa 2 __/__ __/__ __/__ __/__
  MasterCard 1 __/__ __/__ __/__ __/__
  MasterCard 2 __/__ __/__ __/__ __/__
  American Express __/__ __/__ __/__ __/__
  DiscoverCard __/__ __/__ __/__ __/__
  Gas Card 1 __/__ __/__ __/__ __/__
  Gas Card 2 __/__ __/__ __/__ __/__
  Dept. Store Card 1 __/__ __/__ __/__ __/__
  Dept. Store Card 2 __/__ __/__ __/__ __/__
  Finance Co. 1 __/__ __/__ __/__ __/__
  Finance Co. 2 __/__ __/__ __/__ __/__
  Credit Line __/__ __/__ __/__ __/__
  Student Loan 1 __/__ __/__ __/__ __/__
  Student Loan 2 __/__ __/__ __/__ __/__
  Other _____ __/__ __/__ __/__ __/__
  Other _____ __/__ __/__ __/__ __/__
  Other _____ __/__ __/__ __/__ __/__
  Other _____ __/__ __/__ __/__ __/__
  Other _____ __/__ __/__ __/__ __/__

IRREGULAR INCOME PLANNING

Many of us have irregular incomes. If you are self-employed as I am or work on commission or royalties, then planning your expenses is difficult since you cannot always predict your income. You should still do all the Sheets except Sheet 7. Sheet 5 will tell you what you have to earn monthly to survive or prosper and those real numbers are very good for goal setting.

What you must do is to take the items on Sheet 5 and prioritize them by importance. I mean by *importance*, not *urgency*. You should ask yourself, " If I only have enough money to pay one thing, what would that be." Then ask, " If I only have enough money to pay one more thing, what will that be." and so on down the list. Now be prepared to stand your ground because things have a way of seeming important that are only urgent. Saving should be a high priority.

The third column, "Cumulative Amount, " is total of all amounts above that item. So if you get a $2,000 check you can see how far down your priority list you can go.

Item	Amount	Cumulative Amount

BREAKDOWN OF SAVINGS

As you save for certain items like furniture, car replacement, home maintenance, or clothes your savings balance will grow. This sheet is designed to remind you that all that money is committed to something, not just a Hawaiian vacation on impulse because you are now "rich." Keep up with your breakdown of savings monthly here for one quarter at a time.

ITEM	BALANCE BY MONTH:		
Emergency Fund(1)	_____	_____	_____
Retirement Fund	_____	_____	_____
College Fund	_____	_____	_____
Real Estate Taxes	_____	_____	_____
Homeowners Ins.	_____	_____	_____
Repairs or Mn. Fee	_____	_____	_____
Replace Furniture	_____	_____	_____
Car Insurance	_____	_____	_____
Car Replacement	_____	_____	_____
Disability Insurance	_____	_____	_____
Health Insurance	_____	_____	_____
Doctor Bills	_____	_____	_____
Dentist	_____	_____	_____
Optometrist	_____	_____	_____
Life Insurance	_____	_____	_____
School Tuition	_____	_____	_____
School Supplies	_____	_____	_____
Gifts (inc. Christmas)	_____	_____	_____
Vacation	_____	_____	_____
Other _____	_____	_____	_____
Other _____	_____	_____	_____
Other _____	_____	_____	_____
Other _____	_____	_____	_____
Other _____	_____	_____	_____
Other _____	_____	_____	_____
Other _____	_____	_____	_____
TOTAL	_____	_____	_____

THE DEBT SNOWBALL

List your debts in descending order with the smallest payoff or balance first. Do not be concerned with interest rates or terms unless two debts have similar payoffs, then list the higher interest rate debt first. Paying the little debts off first shows you quick feedback and you are more likely to stay with the plan.

Redo this sheet each time you pay off a debt so you can see how close you are getting to freedom. Keep the old sheets to wallpaper the bathroom in your new debt free house. The "new payment" is found by adding all the payments on the debts listed above that item to the payment you are working on, so you have compounding payments which will get you out of debt very quickly. Number is the number of payments left .

Date:_____ Count down to freedom

Item	Total Payoff	Payment	New Payment	Number	Account #

The Lampo Group Products

The Lampo Group offers a 90-day satisfaction guarantee on all our products. If you are not satisfied that the information contained in our products or the quality of presentation was not worth what you paid for it we will give you a 100% refund (minus shipping & handling). We ask that you return the product undamaged and specify your area of dissatisfaction.

Financial Peace **Book** **12.95**

Financial Peace **Gift Books** - **10 or more** ....**each 9.00**
These also make great client gifts! - **30 or more** ....**each 7.00**

Financial Peace **Book on Tape**..**29.95**
This is the unabridged, word-for-word *Financial Peace* book on 3 audio cassettes.

Money Game **Audio Cassette -**
    45 minutes of the Basics **9.95**
Learn the down-to-earth, common sense rules of how to win at the game of money!

Financial Peace **Seminar on Audio Cassette -**
    Biblical Series...**59.00**
This 6 cassette, 4 hour audio series was taped before a live audience at Bethel Chapel. It includes the Biblical basis for Dave's financial concepts, and comes with an accompanying workbook and cash flow system.

Financial Peace **Seminar on Audio Cassette** **49.00**
This 6 cassette, 4 hour series is divided into 8 thirty minute sections for easy learning and retention. It was recorded before a live studio audience, and takes the listener step-by-step through Dave's financial concepts.

Financial Peace **Seminar on Video**.......................................**98.00**
This series is our crown jewel! It was taped before a live studio audience, as Dave led them through his common-sense financial principles. The 2 VHS video cassettes contain 8 thirty minute sessions, over 4 hours, and are accompanied by the workbook and cash flow system. This life-changing financial resource is well worth the investment, and will bring the diligent student immense returns!

Order Form

Product Description	Quantity	Price
TN residents only, add 8.25% sales tax		
For shipping please add 5% ($2 minimum)		
Total Price		

If you have any questions or comments, please call us at **(615) 361-6411**. Please make checks payable to **The Lampo Group**. Send your check and completed order form to:

The Lampo Group
P. O. Box 17708
Nashville, TN 37217

Thank - you!